FINDING THE RIGHT JOB

FINDING THE RIGHT JOB

Anne Segall with William Grierson

BBC BOOKS

Published by BBC Books,
a division of BBC Enterprises Limited,
Woodlands, 80 Wood Lane, London W12 0TT

First published 1990
Reprinted 1991
Revised edition 1994

ISBN 0 563 37104 8

Set in 10/13 pt Meridien by
Phoenix Photosetting, Chatham, Kent

Printed in England by Clays Ltd, St Ives plc
Cover printed by Clays Ltd, St Ives plc

Contents

Acknowledgements

We are delighted that *Finding the Right Job* is being published in this second edition. It has given us the opportunity to update much of our original material and to include an extended reference section as well as additional space for job searchers to keep a record of their applications.

Once again, we wish to thank our many clients whose experiences and ideas have contributed to every aspect of this book. They are continuing to put our theory of job searching into practice, and we are both delighted with their successes and grateful to them for their feedback.

Our colleagues at the BBC and in the wider, professional field of career management have also encouraged us along the way and we are indebted to them for their contributions. Thanks must also go to the staff of BBC Books who have kept faith with us during many rewrites and redrafts.

Last but certainly not least we would, once again, like to thank our respective partners, families and friends for their encouragement, support and patience while this second edition was being prepared, particularly as we promised them last time that it would never happen again!

Finally, we hope that you, the reader, will find this book useful and that, above all, it helps you find the job that is right for you.

Anne Segall and William Grierson

July 1994

Introduction

Seventy-five per cent of candidates do poorly in interviews and feel anxious about them not because they are unsuitable for the job but because they lack the necessary interview skills.

Recruiters say that unsuccessful candidates are the ones who drift into their offices without any apparent preparation and only the vaguest idea of what they are going to say!

The majority of job seekers have never seen a well-presented CV let alone written one.

To many job seekers the hidden job market remains hidden so they are never able to tap this rich source of new contacts and opportunities.

For those people who are not familiar with the process of changing jobs these are just a small sample of the hurdles which need to be overcome. *Finding the Right Job* has been written to help you overcome these and the many other problems which are associated with the whole spectrum of job change.

The book includes information on all aspects of the job search from writing your initial application form to making the right impression at interview. It provides a practical approach, explaining what action is necessary at each stage and helping you decide on the best way to find the job that is right for you.

Many successful job searchers say that changing their job was the best move they made and the job-searching period was a valuable opportunity to evaluate their careers, and so broaden themselves and their horizons. *Finding the Right Job* will show you how to devise your own job-search action plan and help you develop and maintain a positive attitude throughout your job search. By doing this you will soon discover that finding the right job isn't as elusive as you once thought.

1

Your job search

You are looking for a new job. Perhaps you are bored with your present one and want promotion, a salary increase or a new challenge with a different company. Maybe you are redundant, unemployed or have had a career break and now wish to return to full or part-time work. Whatever the reason, embarking on a successful job search is no easy matter. It takes a great deal of effort and hard work to achieve your goal, especially if you want to obtain *the right job* and not just any job.

The world of work has changed dramatically in recent years and will continue to do so in the future. So it will help if we begin by looking at the environment you will be job searching in.

Setting the scene

No one can live their life without being affected by social, economic and political events. So in contemplating your job search you must be aware of factors which will affect the opportunities open to you.

There are two main factors, operating at present, which will affect your choice of future employment.

1 There will be more jobs available in the new technology and service industries and less in the manufacturing sector.

2 By the end of the decade there will be a third fewer school-leavers and graduates available to take up employment.

Interpretation and effects

Fewer jobs will be available in the manufacturing sector, as we move towards the end of the millennium, because of the acceleration in the use of new technology. As more and more companies take up more sophisticated forms of automation and computerisation fewer employees are needed.

The move towards this new technology has grown during the 1990s, particularly since 1992 when our European competitors have entered the UK market, promoting their products and ideas. However, as jobs move out of the manufacturing sector new jobs are created in the service or new technology sectors such as computer-aided design, banking, insurance, leisure industries, management consultancies and public relations. This continuing trend has obvious implications for your job search. If, for example, your skills are traditionally based you may have to think about retraining. If you have been a manager or specialist worker with a large manufacturing company, you will need to consider learning new skills and perhaps change your career direction. On the other hand, you may be able to enhance the skills you already have and work for a smaller company (who will, no doubt, wish you to perform more than one function) or for a consultancy which offers expert advice to other companies in their field.

Where previously companies used to promise careers for life and the security that went with it, there are now no such guarantees. A school-leaver today can expect to have between five and ten different jobs in their lifetime, interspersed with periods of unemployment or retraining. The emphasis in the world of work has moved from one of being employed by one company to having the *employability* to be employed by many companies.

Indeed the whole concept of careers has changed as employment patterns have changed. A career used to be seen as progression up a single ladder from apprenticeship to retirement. The longer you worked with a company and the more knowledge and experience you gained, the higher you went. This traditional concept has now been overtaken and replaced by a much wider definition of the concept of a career. So, it's certainly worth reflecting on what a career means to you as you embark on your job search because your view will certainly have an effect on the type and level of job you now take on.

Broadly speaking a career can be seen in four different ways.

1 The traditional, vertical career

If you see yourself progressing up a professional ladder in your working life, you may well have to move from company to company to take on more senior positions. Many companies are now less hierarchical than they were and flatter structures mean there are fewer opportunities to progress upwards. It will also be important to keep acquiring new skills and knowledge in your area of work so that neither you nor your experience becomes redundant.

2 The horizontal career

As it becomes more and more difficult (and to many, less appealing) to move upwards at work, many individuals are now embarking on a series of jobs which link to give them a horizontal career. These jobs may be in different sectors of the market (public or private) and may encompass a variety of companies and geographical locations. Each job may require different skills and knowledge which build on those already acquired. The emphasis here is on movement across jobs and occupational boundaries, not on advancement up a particular professional ladder.

3 The cyclical career

For many individuals the concept of staying in one area of work for all of their paid working life is far too limiting. A cyclical career, therefore, embraces variety in employment. It can include many different jobs which require different levels of knowledge, skill and experience. It may also rely on having more than one paid job at one time. There is no such thing as a typical cyclical career but one might include: two years as an accountant, followed by retraining as a psychiatric nurse (while working part-time as a restaurant manager) for three years, then going into social work and finally taking up a hobby as paid employment and becoming a market gardener. At each stage the individual takes their previous knowledge, skills and experience and transfers and markets them towards the new opportunity they have decided upon.

4 The steady state career

In this instance an individual remains in their job for the majority of their working life. Usually this job would be in a vocational area such as teacher, nurse, doctor, etc. It may also be someone who has had a previous career and has now settled into self-employment having started and maintained their own business. While it is still possible to undertake a steady state career, it is not as 'steady' as it once was and further training to acquire new skills will often be the order of the day if an individual wishes to stay in a post.

....

Each of these career types has obvious implications for your forthcoming job search, and above all you must make sure that any new job gives you the additional experience, training and skills which you can take with you to future employers. It's also important to look after your finances, investing wisely and taking out pension and other investment plans to protect against possible periods of unemployment or retraining.

Grants and loans are now available to help you retrain and the reference section at the back of this book will help you get started if this is the course of action you need to pursue.

Further developments

The last twenty years have also seen a successful challenge by women to their traditional role. More and more women have sought the personal and financial rewards that are available in the work-place and they are steadily taking an increasing share of the labour market. This is particularly important when looking at the demographic trend mentioned earlier. As fewer young people are available for work, companies will try to fill their vacancies with women who have had career breaks, perhaps to bring up young families. Enlightened employers are starting to offer financial help towards childcare and work-place nurseries to encourage female staff back to work. When job searching you should check which facilities a company offers its employees and what you may be able to negotiate for.

Work to live or live to work?

With these changes in work-trends have come changes in our social and leisure activities. Many UK companies now offer more flexible working patterns which recognise that many people can and do want to balance their life style more equally between work and home. Some service-industry jobs now give you the opportunity to work as a home-based consultant and schemes such as flexitime, job sharing and phased retirement are becoming more and more popular.

While the foregoing holds true as a general summary, in some companies the picture can look quite different. Rather than working more flexibly, cutbacks and redundancy have led many organisations to ask for more from their existing and new employees in terms of job content and hours worked. So, when beginning your job search, work out what your negotiating position is in terms of hours, overtime and location of work. Next, find out exactly what a company is offering in terms of conditions of employment and what plans they have or are developing for their future working practices.

If they offer you a job you can then negotiate with them to ensure you have a package which suits you, your family and your new employer.

Types of work

If the future is going to hold periods of unemployment and retraining, you will need to consider how to market your time away from work positively when attending a job interview. The answer, in this situation, is to forget the traditional concept of work. Instead divide your time into periods of *paid* and *unpaid* work.

Work
••••••••••••

Paid
A job for which you are given an agreed salary. It may be a job which is intrinsically rewarding or one which you would not choose to do unless you needed the money.

Unpaid
An activity you enjoy or feel is useful, and which you do for no other reason than personal or social fulfilment. For example, acting as secretary to a residents' association, organising a local drama group or fund-raising for a favourite charity. Unpaid work can also cover an activity you do not enjoy, but are obliged to do by agreement or necessity. For example, gardening in your block of flats, or DIY in the home.

The skills you exhibit are equally valid whether they are used for paid or unpaid work. As long as you match your skills to those needed for a vacancy or training opportunity, you will be able to market yourself successfully at an interview. This model also holds true for those who have taken a career break or have been unemployed for some time.

Health Check
....

It is now worth taking some time to consider how you are feeling about your job search.

If it is you who is instigating the change, you may feel elated and excited at the opportunities which may be waiting for you. However, if you have lost your job through redundancy or for some other reason, you may be feeling bitter, unwanted and lacking in confidence. You may also experience financial problems and a lack of security which add to your worries. If you are returning to paid work after some time away, the prospect may also seem quite daunting, whether you have been looking after your family, been ill, been caring for someone else or are returning to work after a period of retraining. Whatever the reason for your lack of confidence it is vitally important that you approach your job search with a positive attitude. It has often been said that looking for a job is a job in itself and so before starting you must feel up to the challenge both physically and mentally.

Depending on your circumstances a new set of clothes, a new haircut or that portable computer you need, may be just the thing to put you in the right frame of mind to get you started. However, you may require more specialised help and support, particularly if you have been through a painful redundancy situation. Even though you know it is the post and not you as an individual that is redundant, the feelings of rejection and abandonment can remain for many years. It is, therefore, crucial that you get professional help if your subsequent job search is to be a successful one. Trying to search for a job when you are feeling depressed will doubtless lead to failed interviews which in turn will only exacerbate the situation. Sometimes people believe that it is a weakness to ask for help, but this is most certainly not the case and there are trained professionals available who can offer the support and advice that you need during a period of job change. For further information look in the reference section at the back of this book or, if you are currently in employment, contact your local personnel or welfare manager.

Finding the right job has never been simple and, as previously outlined, trends indicate that this will continue to be the case. But, however bad the employment situation appears, don't be tempted to take on just any job or the first job you are offered because you are worried about being unemployed. Taking a job that does not match your skills and interests will leave you and your employer disillusioned and demotivated.

Do your homework, have some professional

work counselling if you need it, undergo retraining if necessary, and prepare thoroughly to find the job that is right for you. Waiting that little bit longer and preparing that bit more rigorously will pay untold dividends in the longer run.

To help you begin thinking about the best way forward, take some time to answer the following questions. If you can't complete them on your own ask a friend, partner or counsellor for some help. The answers you give will help you focus on what you really want your job search to achieve.

Questions

1 Do I want to continue in the same sort of work and is it possible for me to do so?

2 Do I want a new job in a similar area of work?

3 Do I want to do something completely different?

4 Do I want to work for myself?

5 Do I need to update my knowledge or learn new skills for a new career?

6 Do I need to build my confidence before I begin my job search and if I do, who can support me in this?

The answers to these questions should help you fill in the following work plan. You don't need to be very specific at this stage, but it will help if you provide yourself with an outline. Remember, once you begin to research you can always come back and amend your plan. Committing yourself on paper is a very important step in your job search and you should take the opportunity to write down your thoughts and ideas whenever you can.

My Proposed Work Plan

I want to change my job to

I want to return to paid work as

I want to train as

To do this I will need to

The advantage for me and my family is

The difficulties/disadvantages for me and my family are

It is very important at this stage that you look at the potential advantages and disadvantages of your desired work situation. Taking charge of your job search and making it what you want is a major step in your life and you must be aware of the reality it will bring both for you and for those closest to you. For example, taking a further education course may result in better job prospects, but are you certain that you, and those nearest to you, can cope with the time and finance additional study requires? Likewise, taking a similar job with another company may seem advantageous to begin with, but how long will it be before you become bored and lose interest? If this were the case, what knock-on effects would another job search have for you, your family and friends?

Whatever the case, it is important at this stage not to make any rash decisions. Consider all options and discuss your plans widely before committing yourself to a course of action. This is especially important if you are thinking of retraining or taking a course in further education. It will take the same job-searching skills and as much effort to secure a place on a course as it will to undertake a full job search. It will also take just as much effort to complete a course as it does to hold down a new job. Further training or education should, therefore, never be seen as an easy way of avoiding real work but as a way of enhancing your existing knowledge and skills or gaining new ones.

Having taken stock of your current situation you are ready to begin your job search.

Beginning your job search

You may be job searching while in full-time employment or while unemployed or on a career break. Whichever is the case it is important to establish a routine as soon as you can and to stick to it.

If possible you should set aside a space at home where you can work from. Make sure you have a good supply of stationery and folders for copies of your CV, application forms and covering letters. The sooner you establish a routine the easier your job search will become. It will also give you a framework for the day if you are no longer at work. Your daily or weekend routine should include:

▶ visiting the local library to look at trade and professional magazines and catch up on the latest adverts in the national and local papers.
▶ preparation for any interviews that may be coming up.
▶ writing speculative letters and making applications.

Award yourself treats when you feel you have achieved something positive, for example completing and posting an application form. If you let yourself drift, you will soon become demotivated. Try not to let your worries destroy either family or social life and don't ignore leisure activities; they help keep you in a positive frame of mind for your job search.

It is equally necessary that your family and friends realise how important your job-searching routine is. Share your triumphs and failures with them but try if you can to choose moments when they feel able to listen fully.

If you are unemployed or redundant you will probably be at home a great deal more, and you must respect other people's living and working routines. Remember, they may not be used to having you around. It's important, therefore, that you work out a joint plan to help with increased chores and still put real effort into your job search.

Action planning

You are now ready to embark on your job search.

Begin by listing on a large sheet of paper *all* your skills and abilities. In the left-hand column write details of your employment, education, training and leisure activities. Against each topic write answers to the following questions:

What do I actually do in terms of paid and unpaid work?

What responsibilities do I have?

Who am I responsible to and for?

What do I enjoy doing the most and the least?

What abilities do I have?

What achievements have I had?

If you find this difficult to do alone, ask a supportive partner, friend or colleague to help you. It's surprising what they will include that, through false modesty, you will have missed! Check that you have included *everything*. The exercise will result in a data-bank of information about yourself. You will be able to draw on this to complete application forms, letters and your CV. It will also help you extract information about yourself relevant to individual vacancies.

What do you want?

When you have completed the above exercise you should have a better idea of the skills, qualifications and experience you can offer a potential employer. You are now ready to analyse the sort of job you want in some detail.

You should consider:

a Job content
   think of the functions you know well and the tasks you are experienced in carrying out.

b Status
   what level of responsibility are you looking for? Do you want a job that will lead to a future senior management position or simply increased job satisfaction? Which is more important, financial reward or job fulfilment?

c Salary
   what is the minimum you need to keep up important or essential aspects of your life style?

d Location
   discuss with, and consider the needs of, mem-

bers of your family who will be affected by any decision you might make on moving.

e Prospects

how ambitious are you? How hard are you prepared to work at furthering your career? For example, are you the sort of person who would move home if you were offered a promotion or work long hours perhaps at the expense of your family and social life?

It is important to be realistic about your prospects and the time it can take to find a new job. You may have to make many applications before you get an interview or job offer. But whilst being realistic and frank with yourself about any weak points, make sure you also recognise every asset you can offer a prospective employer.

Often something which at first sight looks like a weakness can in fact be a strength. Remember, age means experience and can be a strong selling point to the right employer. And while doing a specialised job for a long time with the same company may not be a recommendation to an employer looking for broad experience, to an employer in your own field, your background may be worth its weight in gold.

Remember you are entering a *job market* where you will have to *sell* yourself. Your strengths, experience, skills and achievements are your *selling point*.

Sources of job vacancies

By now you will have considered your own abilities and the type of job you would like. The time has now come to look for vacancies.

1 You should answer advertisements in the national, local or specialised press and also consider placing your own advertisement. Newspapers are available at your local library.

When you see the advertisement which describes just the job you are looking for, resist the temptation to send a photocopy of your CV under cover of a letter which adds very little to the information offered. Your aim should be to make inclusion in the shortlist for interview a likely event. This can be done if you proceed as follows.

Carefully read the information in the advertisement regarding:

Conditions of employment	Personal attributes
Type of candidate sought	Experience required
Qualifications	Job specifications
Special skills	Interests

and list what you consider to be the employer's main needs.

Write your covering letter highlighting those needs, saying briefly how you satisfy them and drawing attention to that part of your CV which provides the supporting evidence. CVs and covering letters are considered in detail in Chapters 2 and 3.

If the company asks you to complete an application form phrase the information you give in accordance with the wording in the original advert. Again include a covering letter and remember to keep a copy for future reference.

2 Send your CV to personnel recruitment agencies listed in the *Yellow Pages* or contact your local library. They will look for openings on your behalf if they feel they have a chance of placing you.

3 Call on suitable local employment agencies.

4 Approach any professional organisation to which you belong.

5 See whether your present work contacts can make any introductions on your behalf.

6 Ensure that all your friends, acquaintances and contacts (both private and business) know you are looking for a job. If they cannot employ you directly they may know of suitable openings.

7 Approach companies at conferences and marketing events.

8 Identify potential employers who have not advertised and write them a speculative letter. Ask if they will see you for a general interview to discuss their company and future vacancies. Marketing yourself in this way keeps you ahead of the competition. The approach also gives you the initiative, as you decide which organisations, sectors, jobs and areas most interest you. Speculative approaches are dealt with in detail in Chapter 5.

Thinking About Self-employment?

You may have decided that you no longer want to work for an organisation, and that it would suit you much better if you were to become self-employed. This might be as a freelancer in your current or a new profession, or by starting up your own company or small business.

Increasingly this is an option taken up by many people and the attractions are obvious. You are your own boss and have the responsibility to make decisions. You can choose your own hours of work and are no longer responsible to anyone else for what you decide to do. In theory it can sound to some like the dream solution. In practice this can turn out to be far from the case.

Self-employment is not the easy alternative to conducting a thorough job search, and only those who are really clear about what they are going to do and how they are going to achieve it have any real chance of succeeding. Even then many new businesses collapse every year and you should, therefore, research very thoroughly before making self-employment your preferred option.

If you think self-employment might be the right path for you, have a look at the following questions and talk them over with your partner, friends and those who can give you professional advice. Do you have answers to each of the questions listed and do you fully appreciate the implications your answers carry both for you and for those closest to you?

1 What are you going to sell – is it yourself or is it a product?

2 Is there room in the market place for you or your product? Have you carried out your research actively and thoroughly?

3 Are you considering setting up on your own, with someone else or as a limited company – and do you really understand the business, financial and tax positions of each of these options?

4 Once you are established, how are you going to price yourself and conduct your business?

5 How are you going to advertise and market yourself?

6 Do you know how to compile and write an effective and convincing business plan? Bank managers and accountants will need evidence that your business idea is sound and viable before they take you on as a client or lend you money to start up your business.

7 Have you considered, and do you (or someone close to you who you can trust) understand the financial aspects of being self-employed such

as: taxation, national insurance, VAT and the account-keeping that underpins any new business venture?

8 Have you thought what it would be like *not* to have a regular income, to work hard and yet forgo holidays and can you arrange cover if you are sick – even for a few days?

9 What will the effect of self-employment be on your family and friends? Have you considered the long hours and possible time away from home you will almost certainly have to put in? If you are starting a business, are you expecting your family and friends to get involved and, if you are, will they be able to fit your work in with their other responsibilities?

10 How much capital do you have to venture and where are your boundaries? For example, will you have to put your house up as collateral, take a loan or use all of a redundancy payment? Whichever is the case it is important to think of the potential consequences if you make a continued loss.

It is also useful to talk to other people who have set up on their own, particularly if they are in the same or a related field. Ask them what went well for their business and what have been the pitfalls – particularly in the first year.

Self-employment for many people has turned out to be a rewarding, enjoyable and profitable option. Many individuals look back and wonder how they ever handled a regular work routine which always included answering to someone else. For others, however, the dream of a small business has turned into a nightmare and they have ended up losing not just their initial capital but often their house, health, family and friends.

So, perhaps above all others, this is an option which needs to be considered most carefully. And if having studied the list above you think it may well be the right one for you, then you may wish to contact the addresses at the end of this book where you will be able to obtain help and advice on becoming self-employed.

First steps to the right job option

Whether you wish to become self-employed or are going to pursue a career with an established company you will need a professional and well-presented CV. This will outline your experience and your potential to prospective interviewers or employers – be they the bank manager, from whom you will need to secure your first loan, or the recruiter at the organisation to which you wish to apply. CVs and application forms are dealt with in detail in the next chapter.

2

....

Curriculum vitae
and application forms

A curriculum vitae (CV), often referred to as a personal history form or career résumé, is the accepted, professional way of presenting your personal details on paper to an employer. Its purpose is to ensure that they quickly identify you as a potential candidate for a vacant position and so add your name to the list of people they wish to interview.

Your CV has to do a very important job on your behalf and so it's vital that you make it as positive and attractive as you possibly can. It should be brief (if it's longer than two sides of A4 the recruiter may not take the trouble to read through it), accurate and well thought out. It must also clearly list your strengths and achievements, showing what you have done and how well you have done it.

Your CV
....

Some sources say that you should write a new CV for each job you apply for. This gives you the opportunity to angle your previous experience to the vacancy on offer. If you have the time and resources this is a good idea, providing, of course, that you remember which version of your CV you have sent to which employer! However, few people have the capacity to produce several documents at once and if you are applying for two or three jobs each week, or a number of training opportunities you need to think seriously about the time and effort needed to complete several versions of your CV. A well-planned CV should take you 1–2 days to write and have word-processed, and it may be impractical to finish it in time to meet an advertised closing date, especially if someone else is wordprocessing it for you.

The solution to this problem is to have one CV which covers your career history in a general but positive way and then to include a *covering letter*, which states why you are specifically suited for the vacancy. Covering letters are dealt with later in this chapter and in more detail in Chapter 3.

Design
....

The design of your CV, that is the layout and the information you include in it, is dependent on both your personal preference and, more particularly, on the type of work you are looking for.

Different CVs suit different situations and you should, therefore, choose the one that is right for you and for your circumstances.

There are three main ways of presenting the information in your CV, listed below.

1 Chronological

You should use a Chronological CV if you are applying for a job in the same field as your previous or current job. This is the traditional CV and it is particularly good at:

▶ reviewing your career and employment history to date.

▶ selling your work-record and history of achievements.

▶ identifying your main duties and responsibilities for each of the jobs you have held.

A Chronological CV allows an employer to see immediately what experience you have had in a particular job and which skills and knowledge you will, therefore, bring to the new company.

2 Functional

A Functional CV concentrates not so much on previous jobs but on the skills you wish to market. It is particularly useful if:

▶ you are changing companies or location and wish to emphasise particular skills to a new recruiter.

▶ you are applying for retraining and need to focus on tasks you have undertaken rather than on job titles.

3   Predictive

A Predictive or future-focused CV is similar to a Functional CV in that it concentrates on the skills and knowledge you have to market rather than on jobs you have had. However, the aim of this CV is to launch you to an entirely new career or area of work rather than to similar work in another company. It begins with an aim or objective and then all the supporting information you give is used to back the outlined aim. It is very useful:

▶ for conveying an impression of someone who knows what they want and is proactively setting out to create an opportunity for themself.

▶ for those in the freelance market, testifying to their previous experience and setting out their goals for future work.

Layout
················

The following examples show you the three alternative CV layouts. You will probably have a preferred style which you will want to follow but above all don't lose sight of the content of your CV and how it markets you. The content is every bit as important as the typeface or layout you select. For example, there would be little point in sending a Chronological CV to an employer in a completely new area of work. The CV would give them the details of your past experience but would not show how you intend bringing that past experience to bear on your future work. So, think carefully before drafting your document and, whichever form you choose, do make sure that it is clearly typed and well presented.

Example 1 – Chronological CV

....

CURRICULUM VITAE

SUMMARY
Insert summary of experience in this space. For example:

I am a qualified and experienced electrician with supervisory and practical skills gained from many years of working within a complex technical environment.

NAME   :

ADDRESS   :

TELEPHONE NO.   :   DAY:
                      EVENING:

(if you wish, include)
DATE OF BIRTH   :   AGE:

EMPLOYMENT HISTORY:
(start with current or last job and work back)

....

DATE   COMPANY ADDRESS

<u>POSITION:</u>   (e.g. Salesman, Engineer,
Warehouse Manager, Senior
Accounts Supervisor)

<u>DUTIES:</u>

DATE   COMPANY ADDRESS

<u>POSITION:</u>

<u>DUTIES:</u>
(continue as above and work back to your first job, giving more gener-
alised details of your duties each time)

<u>TRAINING:</u>

<u>EDUCATION:</u>

DATE   COLLEGE/UNIVERSITY
(if applicable)

DATE   SENIOR SCHOOL

<u>QUALIFICATIONS:</u>

<u>INTERESTS AND HOBBIES:</u>

<u>ADDITIONAL INFORMATION:</u>
e.g.
Available for immediate interview.
Date of birth and age (if not included on first page).
Full driving licence.
Willing to work in UK and abroad.
Willing to relocate (state areas).

Example 2 – Functional CV

NAME   :

ADDRESS   :

TELEPHONE NO.   : DAY:
                         EVENING:

PROFILE:
Give a brief summary (5 lines maximum) of who you are and the position you require. For example:

I am an enthusiastic and very experienced Personal Assistant with full administrative and customer care skills acquired within the public sector, now looking to broaden my experience within the financial sector.

Main Skills and Experience
Highlight all skills associated with being a per-sonal assistant – including administrative and customer care skills. In particular, emphasise all experience and knowledge connected with the financial sector. This will mean giving a short description of each skill and how it enhances your ability to perform your role at work.

Achievements
Again, highlight the main achievements you have had of posts held previously. Following the example here, you would emphasise any achievements which include a financial aspect.

Employment History
Briefly list your employment history in chronological order – starting with your current or most recent post. There is no need to give too much detail here, as you will have included this under the skills and achievements sections.

Education
List qualifications gained at University/College/School.

Courses
List relevant training courses – again, following the example, those with financial emphasis would be cited first.

Additional Information
List main interests and other relevant information not included above.

Example 3 – Predictive CV
• •

(CENTRE) Your name and your contact number

(CENTRE) A brief summary of the work/position you are seeking, for example:

I am looking for a management position which will build on my previous experience where I have developed extensive counselling and training experience.

(CENTRE) Your address

Date of birth and age (if you wish to include them)

Main skills and experience in support of my application for the position of

• • • • • • • • • • • • • •

List here all your relevant skills and achievements from paid and unpaid work which contribute to your aim of securing the position outlined in your summary.

Qualifications and Training in support of my application
for the position of

List here the qualifications and training you have had which are relevant to the position you are aiming for – leave out those which are not applicable.

Employment record

Briefly list your employment to date – give added detail on those jobs which contribute to the position you wish to secure.

Interests

List interests and membership of organisations; again, with your goal in mind, list only those which are relevant.

Education

List as on previous examples.

Additional information

There should be less additional information, if any, on the Predictive CV as all relevant information should have been included in the previous sections.

For each CV ensure your name and contact number appear at the bottom of each sheet.

Having decided on your layout think carefully about which titles you want to emphasise and which details can go in lower-case letters. Use the full range of capitals, lower case letters, underlinings and emboldened type to make your CV look as attractive as possible. Don't be tempted to overdo it however!

Too many emboldened titles or versions of typeface will make the document harder to read and will, therefore, distract the recruiter. The rule is to *keep your CV clear and simple*.

Compilation
....

You are now ready to consider the information that needs to be included on your CV.

Write down the points of information required in each category, making sure you have the correct dates, job titles and addresses to hand. Next, develop details of your employment history in an effective and positive way, avoiding jargon and abbreviations used by your present or previous employer which will mean nothing to recruiters in other organisations.

The data from the Action Plan you completed in Chapter 1 will also help you to give clear and precise details of your position and duties, while showing a potential employer the skills you have and how you have been successful. Remember, if a potential employer reads of your success in your previous job they are going to want to interview you to see if you can bring the same success to their company.

You should make use of the action verbs listed below to illustrate your strengths, as these will give the recruiter a positive picture of you. But do take care to use them selectively: you don't want to sound too good to be true!

Action verbs

accomplished
approved
assisted
authorised
budgeted
compiled
completed
composed
conceived
consulted
controlled
dealt with
delivered
demonstrated
designed
developed

established
estimated
expanded
explained
finalised
guided
implemented
initialled
instructed
introduced
learned
managed
motivated
negotiated
organised
participated

performed
planned
prepared
promoted
reorganised
researched
scheduled
set up
solved
strengthened
supervised
trained
utilised
wrote

In general you should consider including the following information in each section.

Personal details
Enter your full name and preferred title, home address, telephone numbers (day and evening),

age and date of birth. Some older applicants prefer to include their age and date of birth at the end of their CV under Additional Information. This ensures that the recruiter reads about an individual's positive attributes without having first seen their age; it is felt that this can help rule out the possibility of age discrimination. In the end this is very much a personal choice and as potential age barriers vary from industry to industry and from company to company, it is impossible to set any hard and fast rules. However, recruiters *do* become suspicious if age is not included on a CV, and this may stop them from inviting you for an interview.

If you feel there is a chance that your candidature will be prejudiced by your age, you should counter it by making personal contact with the company while your application is being processed, write a good covering letter, speak to as many contacts as you can and try to arrange a visit to the company and informal chat with the recruiter before your interview. If handled positively this will dispel any doubts they may have had about your candidature. The same method can be adopted if you are returning to work after a career break or have been unemployed for a considerable length of time.

Employment details
Start with your current or last job and work back, giving dates of joining and leaving your past employers. You do not need to state salaries at

this stage (unless specifically asked to do so) or say why you left one job for another.

Next, list the companies, and/or departments within companies, you have worked for, with relevant addresses. You mustn't leave gaps of time unaccounted for on your CV, particularly on a Chronological CV, or recruiters will wonder what you were doing in the gaps!

If you've had a period of unemployment or a break from paid work you must still account for your time. Show that you had a career break or a break in employment from . . . to . . . and then in a few lines state the *positive* things you did during this time. For example:

1 From May 1987 to January 1988 I had a career break during which time I learnt word processing and acted as General Secretary for a local charity group. This has improved my skills as an organiser and administrator.

If you are unable to write positively about additional activities during your period of unemployment you could adopt the following example:

2 From May to December 1988 *(insert additional periods of unemployment)* I had an employment break. During this time I was continually job searching with the aim of securing a promotional position/a career change/increased responsibility. I achieved this with *(insert name of company)* in *(month, year)*.

Position – skills and achievements
Write two or three short paragraphs to demonstrate your experience and skills. Identify clearly areas of responsibility. Be precise and positive and highlight any major successes and achievements.

Education
Colleges/universities: List colleges/universities you attended, with relevant dates.
Senior schools: List the schools you attended, with relevant dates.

Qualifications: State qualifications from schools, colleges/universities: examinations taken, grades obtained.

Other training: Put down all relevant courses, especially those that market *you* as an individual i.e., management courses, office administration skills, anything specialised like computers, photography, languages or training involving technical aptitude.

Interests and hobbies
As appropriate, insert at least three topics to demonstrate leisure activities, for example, sports, musical instrument played, voluntary work for a charity etc., membership of clubs or associations, DIY.

If the job you want relies on experience gained from your interests and hobbies rather than your work experience, you may wish to move this section to the front of your CV. For example, your interests are in the field of sports and leisure and you wish to become a sports instructor, but at present work as a computer operator. In this case refer to your sporting interests and achievements immediately after your personal details, following the layout for the Predictive CV.

Additional information
As shown in the example CVs, you may wish to add information here which does not fit into other categories.

Drafting
Once you have compiled the necessary information, type or write your CV in draft form and ask yourself the following questions:

1 Does my CV fit on to two pages of A4-sized paper?

2 Is it neat, tidy and well laid out with no spelling errors? Remember, faced with a mountain of applications employers often jump on wrong spelling and bad grammar as an excuse for rejecting people.

3 Are the names, dates, addresses and telephone numbers correct?

4 Do my employment history description, interests and hobbies do me justice in a positive and concise way?

5 Does my CV tell a potential employer in less than half a minute what my last job was and what I have done in the past?

6 Am I sure that I have not omitted anything important?

7 Have I used terms and words that will be understood by others?

8 Do I feel confident showing my CV to a friend or colleague for approval?

9 Does it tell a prospective employer that I am worth seeing for an interview?

10 Does my CV properly market me?

If the answer to all ten questions is *yes* and you are completely satisfied, have the final document carefully and attractively laid out and typed. Proof-read it thoroughly, then make a number of photocopies for future use.

You should keep your CV up to date. A regular review will ensure that you incorporate relevant new experience or training. Even if your job application is successful, you never know when you may need to apply for another position.

The covering letter – first thoughts

Always include a covering letter with your CV, otherwise there may be little or no indication of what job you're after! It is unrealistic to forward a CV in the hope that a potential employer will try to match your skills to their needs. They don't have the time to do this so you must do the work for them.

The letter should serve as your introduction and give the reason why you are sending your CV, either in response to an advertised vacancy or as a speculative enquiry. If your CV has been structured to be directed at a wide range of employers, the letter is your chance to be specific and highlight any particular attributes you feel you have for the job for which you have applied.

The letter should be as brief as possible – three short paragraphs at most.

1 It should state why you are writing, what position you are interested in, the reference number if applicable and where you saw the vacancy advertised.

   The organisation may be advertising more than one vacancy, or, if you are writing speculatively, the company will need to know the type of vacancy you are looking for.

2 It should then draw the recruiter's attention to your CV and highlight one or two reasons why you are suitable for the job (i.e. 'You will see from my CV that I have X years' experience in . . .').

3 End the letter simply by stating that you look forward to hearing from the company in due

course. There is little to be gained at this stage from waxing lyrical about the company and its product. The longer the letter the less chance it has of being read!

4 Read the letter through before sending it. If you *must* continue on to a second sheet ensure that the last line on the first page does not leave a negative impression. For example:

'...although I have no (*over page*) shortcomings'.

The rule is always to draft your letter before typing or writing the final version. Covering letters are dealt with in more detail in Chapter 3.

Application forms

Irrespective of how effective employers find your CV you will often be requested to complete an application form.

Follow carefully the instructions for application given in the advertisement. If they ask you to 'telephone for a job description and application form', do just that: do not respond by sending a copy of your CV. If you want to get that all-important interview you must take as much time and care with this form as you have in compiling your CV.

Organisations use application forms because it is easier for them to make comparisons between candidates, and it ensures they have all the information they require, which is sometimes omitted from CVs! The rules of presentation and compilation are, however, the same as for CVs.

1 The first thing to do on receiving an application form is to read it through carefully from beginning to end. Make sure you have a copy of your CV beside you and use the information on your CV to help you complete the application form. Follow the instructions carefully, place the requested information in the correct boxes and make sure your dates, spelling and grammar are correct.

2 If you are able to photocopy the form, this can be useful for drafting answers; if not, draft your answers on a separate sheet of paper.

3 Some of the sections of the form will require straightforward, brief and factual answers. Others will require a more detailed response. For example 'What duties did you perform in your last job?' Draft and redraft the detailed answers before completing the final version and if possible angle your answers to key words in the job advertisement. So, for example, if the advert requires 'Good communication and organisational skills', in your answer you should include the information 'My last job used my organisational and communication skills to the full as I was responsible for the general office routine'.

4 Never leave gaps on the form or cram your

answers into too small a space. Presentation is all important. If there is not enough room for your answers, attach another sheet, typed if possible.

5 Certain sections of the application, like 'Any Other Information' are the opportunity for *you* to *sell* your skills, effectiveness and achievements.

6 When you are completely satisfied that you have completed the draft to the best of your ability, write or type out the final version, as requested, checking and rechecking for errors! It is often helpful to have a second person look over your draft answers and the final form.

7 Return the form promptly, by the date requested, and don't forget to keep a copy! This will help you if you are invited for an interview and will save time when completing other applications.

8 Always include a covering letter with your application form. This gives a further opportunity to set your job application apart from other contenders.

Finally
....

Make sure you keep copies of your CV or application form and covering letters so you have a

....

quick reference point when you receive a reply from the company. If you do not hear immediately, don't despair. The company has probably had many replies to its advert and is taking time to sort through them. If, however, you have not heard after a fortnight it is acceptable to make a *polite* phone call to the company to ensure that they received your application. And remember, if you are sending your CV or application form and covering letter in reply to an advertised vacancy make sure you send them off in good time to meet the closing date. If no closing date is given, ensure that your application arrives within ten working days.

3

....

Covering letters

It doesn't matter why you are writing to a company, the rule is always the same; you must carefully prepare your letters to give a good impression of you. Even the letter you write to request an application form must be tidy and well structured. Remember, everything to do with your job application will be put on file and be available at the interview, so a terse note on rough or flowery notepaper simply will not do. It is stupid to prejudice your chances by adopting a sloppy approach. Right from the outset match your letters to the high standard of your CV and application forms and give the recipient of your letter the impression they are dealing with a confident and professional individual.

Your letters should be clearly addressed to the company or organisation concerned. Your address, the date and the name and address of the company should all appear at the top of the page, together with a reference number if you've been asked to quote one. Whenever possible write to a named individual, as this immediately personalises your application: you are dealing with an individual like yourself, not an entire multinational corporation! If you are writing speculatively the best course of action is to phone through to the company's reception and ask for the name of someone either in personnel or in a senior management position in the department of the company you want to work for. It is very rare for this simple request to be refused, but if it is, write to:

The Recruitment Manager
Name of Firm

and begin your letter 'Dear Sir/Madam'. In this case you should end your letter 'Yours faithfully'. If you are writing to a named individual then you should end your letter 'Yours sincerely'. Use your normal signature and print or type your name underneath, adding Mr, Mrs, Miss or Ms in brackets: this avoids any confusion or irritation on the part of the recipient, who may not be able to decipher your signature!

Use plain writing paper. Some people are prejudiced against lined, coloured, flowery or scented paper; certainly *never* use scrap paper. This is an occasion when you will gain the advantage by being conventional.

The written application is the first obstacle you have to negotiate in getting a job, so if you want the job you must make your application as attractive and clear as you possibly can. It would be a great shame to be turned down because of the tone or layout of your letter, before an employer has had a chance to hear what you have to say in support of your application at an interview.

The write approach

Ideally you should have your letters typed, but if this is not possible make sure you write clearly and legibly. The rule is always to draft your letter before typing or writing the final version. You can then be sure you have given the information required and that you have really done yourself justice in terms of your experience, qualifications and abilities.

It is very tempting to compile an all-purpose letter and send it out to all companies on all occasions. This is the lazy approach and should be avoided! While it is acceptable to have a standard letter asking for an application form (although you must remember to change the reference number each time) or for your speculative approaches, it is *not* permissible when you are writing in reply to a specific, advertised vacancy. If a prospective employer has asked for a letter in support of your application it must be tailored to that organisation. Your aim is to appear as attractive a candidate as possible: remember, the company is likely to receive a number of applications so from the outset you are competing with other candidates whose qualifications may be as good or better than your own. Your abilities, experience and achievements, as outlined in your CV, must be highlighted to match the experience the company is looking for. You must emphasise in your letter those points which make you a particularly good applicant. To do this you must *sell* yourself in a specific way and underline the special contribution you think you can make to the company. Find out what you can about the organisation from the advertisement, the company's own careers literature or sales brochures, and then show in your letter that you have found out something about them.

As with your CV, avoid using jargon and abbreviations. You and your present company understand them – but will anybody else?

Unless the employer asks you for a detailed letter saying why you think your training and background are relevant, keep your letter short and to the point. Remember that whatever you write is likely to form the basis for questions when you get to the interview stage, so don't waffle and pad the letter with impressive-sounding generalisations that you won't be able to back up when you come to be questioned about them! The rule is to be specific. So for example, if the company has asked for computer experience, in your letter write 'I have had experience of the following computer software .... and can program in ....'.

If you can write a letter or indeed fill in a form showing a link between something you have actually done and the job you are applying for the interviewer will have something concrete to ask questions about, giving you a further oppor-

....

tunity for showing just how suitable a candidate you are. What is more important is that you will be able to make a favourable impression because you will have led the interviewer to talk to you about areas you feel confident in.

If you are writing speculatively this rule still applies. You must *sell* yourself on paper. Your relevant qualifications and experience together with a line or two explaining why you are interested in the company and its products and services will ensure that your letter is well received. You should state that you understand there may not be any immediate suitable vacancies but would be glad to be informed if there are. You can also ask the recruiter for an information meeting to obtain general advice; you may well get this. Even if there is no job available a discussion of this sort acts as an introduction and will help in future applications to that company. Speculative approaches are covered in more detail in Chapter 5.

On the following pages you will find examples of the types of letter you may need to send while you are job searching. Study these and then adapt them to your own needs and circumstance.

Write on . . . !

Example 1 – Letter in response to an advertised vacancy enclosing an application form or your standard CV

Your name
Your address
Date

The company's name and address
(plus reference number if quoted
in the advertisement)

Dear (*Name as in the advert or Sir/Madam*)
Please find enclosed my CV/completed
application form in response to your recent
advert in the *Daily XYZ* of the (*date*) for a
. . . . with your company.

You will see from my CV/application form
that I have good . . . . skills and would be
happy liaising with customers and staff at all
levels. My experience in . . . . is also very
relevant because I am trained in word-processing/
computing/management and leadership. I am
also interested in . . . . which I feel would be
an advantage for the post of . . . .

I am interested in ABC Company because
. . . . and was very interested to read of
your plans to . . . . as this is an area of
particular interest to me.

I would very much like to be considered for
the post of . . . . and am available to
attend for interview at any time.

I look forward to hearing from you.
Yours sincerely/faithfully

YOUR SIGNATURE
Your name printed
Enc.

. . . .

The first letters you write will either accompany your returned application form/CV in response to an advertised vacancy or will be sent with your CV as a speculative approach.

Example 2 – Speculative letter to a company asking if it has any vacancies

Your name
Your address
Date

The company's name and address

Dear (*Named person or Sir/Madam*)

Please find enclosed my CV. You will see from my CV that I have . . . . . years' experience with the ABC Company and that my career before this included working in/for . . . as a . . .

I have a wide range of experience including . . . . I am also trained in/have experience of . . . .

I have good communication skills, work well on my own initiative and as a member of a team and am a good administrator and organiser/warehouse manager/retail supervisor etc.

I now wish to broaden my career base and wonder if you are anticipating any suitable

. . . .

vacancies in the near future for which I could be considered. I am extremely interested in (*name of company*) because . . . . and find your plans to . . . . interesting as I have experience of . . . . I look forward to hearing from you.
Yours sincerely/faithfully

YOUR SIGNATURE
Your name printed.
Enc.

If you are returning to work after a career break you could mention this in the last paragraph:

For the last eighteen months I have had a career break during which time I . . . . I now wish to return to full-time/part-time work and wonder if you are anticipating any vacancies in the near future for which I could be considered.

Your letter should then continue as in Example 2 ('I am extremely interested in (*name of company*) . . .').

People often write speculatively to companies because they have seen them advertising other vacancies. If, for example, a company advertises for twenty-five computer operators, they may be expanding and will soon need supervisors and managers. The following letter covers this situation.

. . . .

Example 3 – Speculative letter to a company that has recently advertised vacancies and which might require other categories of staff

Your name
Your address
Date

The company's name and address

Dear (*Named person as mentioned in the advert*)

I was interested to see your recent advert in the *Daily XYZ* for a . . . .

I realise this means that . . . . Company Ltd is expanding and I am therefore writing to ask if you have any openings in . . . . which would suit someone with my qualifications and experience.

I am interested in developing my work in . . . . seeking wider opportunities in . . . . and wonder if your proposed expansion would bring forth openings in this area.

I have been employed as . . . . at . . . . for the past . . . . . years.

I enclose details of my background and of positions held. I have particular interests/experience in . . . . which would appear to be relevant to the work for which your company is known. I am keen to develop the work I have done at . . . . and think I could make a useful contribution in your own . . . . department.

. . . .

I understand that you may not have immediate vacancies in this field; I should however be grateful for any advice you can offer me and hope that I may come and see you or one of your staff. I will ring your office next week to book an appointment.

With many thanks.

Yours sincerely/faithfully

YOUR SIGNATURE
Your name printed.
Enc.

The closing paragraph of Example letter 3 refers to the possibility of an informal interview with a member of the company. An interview of this kind, known as *an information meeting*, has two functions:

1 It is a good way of finding out more about a company and its forthcoming vacancies.

2 It gives you the opportunity to market yourself positively to a potential employer.

Although not widely known, it is in fact common practice for individuals to write to companies requesting information meetings.

Make sure you do your homework on the company before you go to such a meeting and *always* take a copy of your CV with you.

Additionally, there are two primary rules to bear in mind when you write a letter requesting an information meeting.

1 *Never* directly ask for a job. It may embarrass the recruiter who, while they may be willing to talk to you, may not wish to be pinned down on whether or not they have an opening in their company. This is your opportunity to build up a longer-term relationship with a view to securing a position in the future. If you go too fast too soon, you may spoil your chances of ever securing a job with the company. So, although you probably need the job right now, do give these speculative approaches time to mature. It is better to have lots of speculative approaches on the go at one time (between 10–20 is ideal) than to harangue one or two contacts to the point where they wish they had never seen your original letter!

2 Make sure your initial letter sounds friendly, professional and not too pushy. Try asking someone you trust, a friend or partner perhaps, to look it over for you. If they can *honestly* say *they* would see you for a meeting on the strength of it, then it passes the 'acid test' and you can send your letter off with confidence. A well-written letter, which has the right tone, will immediately establish a rapport between you and the person receiving it, which will help set the focus for your subsequent meeting with them.

The meeting itself is dealt with in further detail in

Chapter 5. Example 4, below, shows the type of letter you should be writing to secure your meeting.

Example 4 – Letter requesting an information meeting

> Your name
> Your address
> Date

The company's name and address

Dear (*It is most important that you write to a named person when requesting an information meeting*)

Please find enclosed my CV. You will see from this I am working as a . . . . in the . . . . department of the ABC Company. This has given me experience in . . . . and has established my skills as . . . . I am fully conversant with . . . . and have been trained in . . . .

I now wish to broaden my career base/widen my opportunities in/develop my work in the field of . . . .

Your name has been given to me by a colleague/I saw your name in a recent advert/directory/I was given your name by a colleague of yours at a recent . . . . conference. He/she suggested I write to you to find out more about . . . . as I believe you may well have the sort of position I would be able to make a contribution in.

Would it be possible to have a brief meeting with you some time to discuss . . . . Company Ltd and the types of vacancy that might be suitable for someone with my background? I will ring your office next week to book an appointment.

With many thanks.

Yours sincerely

YOUR SIGNATURE

Your name printed.

Enc.

NB: Do not despair if you are not granted a meeting. This is not a reflection on you; it is simply that the individual is inundated with similar requests. At the very least you may be sent information which will help you with your job search.

Example 5 – Thank-you letter after an information meeting

Your name

Your address

Date

The company's name and address

Dear (*Named person*)

I am writing to thank you for the very useful meeting of (*date*). It was very kind of you

. . . .

to take the time to see me.

I was particularly interested in the expansion of your . . . . department/new training scheme for/new posts in . . . . and the possibility of future vacancies occurring for someone with my background and experience.

Thank you also for retaining my CV and forwarding it to the Personnel Department/Computer Department.

I will now look out for the . . . . advertisements in the *Daily XYZ*/local newspaper/*ABC magazine*, as you suggested, and will make a formal application when I see a suitable vacancy.

Thank you once again for your time and trouble.

Yours sincerely

YOUR SIGNATURE
Your name printed.

The more politely persistent you are in your letter writing the more chance there is of making a good impression and securing the right job.

The ten golden rules of letter writing
. . . .

You will need to write a wide range of letters during your job-searching period. The examples shown will act as a guide, but even if your needs are more specialised and specific you should

. . . .

always follow the *ten golden rules of letter writing*. This will ensure your letters are always written to an acceptable professional standard.

1 Keep your letters short and to the point: you should aim for three or four short paragraphs on one side of A5 or A4 paper.

2 Don't mention the salary you require in your letter unless specifically asked to do so. If you must mention it, always quote a salary range, not a specific figure. This will leave you room for future negotiation.

3 If a reference number was given in an advert make sure you quote it when you reply.

4 However much you want the job don't plead in your letter or sound too pushy.

5 Be polite and confident.

6 Keep your letters neat and tidy. Don't worry if they are not typed as long as they are clearly legible.

7 Ensure all your facts and dates are correct.

8 Make sure there are no spelling mistakes or wrong numbers – especially your telephone number.

9 Under your signature, print or write your full name.

10 Always, *always* keep a copy for future reference.

4

....

Interview success

Your contacts with potential employers will result in invitations to interview. At this stage the employer is seriously interested in you because your CV detailing your experience and achievements have made them feel you might well satisfy the job requirements. You, therefore, need to make a good impression at the interview to give yourself the best possible chance of securing the job. Seventy-five per cent of candidates do poorly in interviews and feel anxious about them *not* because they are unsuitable for the job but because they lack the necessary interview skills. This chapter introduces these skills and helps you develop them. Once you begin to put them into practice you will find that interviews become stimulating and rewarding experiences which will lead you to *interview success* and a firm *job offer*.

First of all it is important to remind yourself of the purpose of the interview. It provides the employer with an opportunity to judge your suitability for the job and assess you in relation to other candidates. It is also your chance to find out more about the job and the company you might be working for.

Pre-interview preparation
....

Researching the organisation
The first essential step towards a successful interview is *preparation* and if you are to succeed this must begin long before you enter the interview room. Recruiters are immediately put off by applicants who drift into their offices without any apparent preparation and only the vaguest idea of what they are going to say! The reason most people give a poor account of themselves is because they are nervous. These nerves are, in fact, a throw-back to our cave-dwelling origins! In the face of danger or uncertainty our ancestors either fought or took flight, so symptoms such as increased breathing rate, sweating and pumping adrenalin to the limbs served them well. However, these classic signs of nerves are not at all useful for the twentieth-century recruitment interview! They make us freeze or become unnecessarily verbose, stumble over our words and appear clumsy and uncoordinated, traits which are guaranteed not to impress company recruiters. There are two ways to overcome these pre-interview nerves.

1 Make sure you prepare thoroughly before the interview. Research the company and its

products, know the name of your interviewer and how to get to the company and above all think about the questions you'll be asked and work out effective answers to them.

2 It may sound obvious but try to *relax*. Once you know something about the company you won't be embarking on a journey into the unknown, so the element of 'fright' will begin to diminish. While you're waiting to go into the interview room take long slow breaths to control your breathing rate. Once this slows down, the other signs of nerves will begin to disappear and you will be able to greet the recruiter in a more relaxed and positive manner.

No matter how many interviews you've had or how many you still have to attend you must be able to convince an interviewer that you are *genuinely* interested in working only for the company that is interviewing you.

Researching the organisation before you attend for interview will, therefore, benefit you in two ways:

1 You will be able to answer questions on the company and your potential role in it. This, in turn, will improve your presentation and ensure you sound confident, organised and motivated.

2 The company will be impressed by the knowledge you display and the effort you have put

into your interview preparation. If you can show them you have worked hard for the interview they will believe you will work hard for the company if they offer you the job.

Begin by building on some basic facts. Does the company manufacture products? If so, what kind of products does it produce, who does it sell to and where are its plants, offices or stores located? Or does this company provide a service, such as banking, retail or marketing? Where is its corporate headquarters? How many branch offices does it have?

If the firm is a public company check the business pages of the national newspapers for information on it and the public library for a copy of its annual report. The best source of information, though, is the company itself. When you are invited for interview ask the company to send copies of its sales and promotional brochures; it will be happy to do so and you will be showing tangible evidence of your interest. Additionally, if you have been sent for interview via an agency you will be able to get further information from your consultant.

The more you know about the company the more you can use this information to achieve the results *you* want.

Analysing the job specification/advert

Now you know about the company it's time to find out the qualities they want from the successful candidate.

Your first task is to read the job advert thoroughly and carefully. It's surprising how many people miss key facts about a job simply because they haven't studied the advert.

Take an A4 sheet of paper and write down the information from the advert regarding:

Conditions of employment

Type of candidate sought

Qualifications

Specialist skills and experience

Personal attributes and interests

Add to the list any information you found from your research regarding the company's environment, product, staffing levels etc. You can now use this data bank as your own marketing tool. Write down how *you* meet the criteria asked for in the advert, especially any responsibilities you have had and general abilities which make you a particularly *good* candidate.

Some companies also issue job descriptions and person specifications. These outline in detail the content and duties of the job and the qualities they expect from the person who will fill the vacancy. If you are not sent these you should phone the company to see if it can supply them. The job description and person specifications will give you useful additional information for your preparation.

You will definitely be asked questions at the

interview on the criteria included in the advert and from the job description and person specifications, if you have them. Make sure you can explain how your experience, abilities, motivation and so on, meet the company's specifications and remember, the better prepared you are the more confident you will appear.

Building your image and identifying your qualities

The marketing approach
An advertiser wouldn't dream of selling a product by saying 'This product is the same as all the others, there's nothing special about it and in fact in certain conditions it doesn't work at all!'

Yet it is amazing how many people go to interviews and say just that! They admit to failures and weaknesses, lack of experience and no real knowledge of the company they're hoping to join. They then become terribly demoralised when they don't get the job.

If the above approach is wrong for marketing products then it's definitely wrong for marketing *you*!

Build your image and your presentation style by concentrating before the interview on a well-thought-out marketing strategy. Begin with:

Product knowledge
Do you know yourself? Can you talk in detail

about your achievements, qualities and skills? Do you know the key dates of projects you have undertaken and courses you have attended? Can you talk with confidence about experiences you have had and responsibilities you have been given? If you can't, write them down and practise talking about them. The more you practise the more confident and convincing you will sound.

Market research
Do you know your customer, that is, the company you are hoping to work for? Ask yourself: what does the company need and how can I provide it?

Packaging and display
Control your presentation during the interview. You need to project confidence and enthusiasm.

Speak clearly and concisely. Don't waffle away from the point and certainly don't give 'one word' answers: you'll make the recruiter work too hard and lose their interest.

Cultivate a firm handshake and look the interviewer in the eye while you are answering questions. Make sure you don't slouch or sit on the edge of your chair fidgeting nervously. Sit down, make yourself comfortable and look interested at all times.

Dress should be appropriate. Your aim is to look well groomed and professional. Don't try to look different; you want to come across as a reliable member of the team. If in doubt, go for a smarter version of how you'll dress for work.

Remember, you want the interviewer to pay attention to you and the qualities you have to offer, so make sure your clothes enhance rather than distract from that message.

Advertising and promotion

Make sure that any contact you have with the company before your interview is polite and positive. Don't be rude to the receptionist or brusque on the phone. If you are writing to the company, ensure that your letter is well presented, and if you are looking round before the interview, concentrate on *public relations*. Be positive and interested in the information you are given and in what is happening around you.

Above all don't undervalue yourself.

Your unique selling point

You are unique. There is a quality about you that no other candidate for the job possesses. Focus on this quality (a position you have held, responsibility you have taken, etc.) and use it as your *unique selling point*.

This will make you stand out from the other candidates and ensure that the recruiter remembers you *apart* from the rest of the field.

Even if you have been away from paid employment for some time, either having a career break or because of unemployment, you still have a *unique selling point*. During your time away from paid work you may have learnt a new skill, for example word processing, computer operations, administration for voluntary groups. Or you may have taken up a new interest such as amateur dramatics, a foreign language or marriage guidance counselling. Any new skill or interest can provide you with your *unique selling point*. Remember, it doesn't have to be something you've been paid for or a complicated project, simply something you're good at that gives you confidence and makes the interviewer remember you.

Preparing for your interview

Know the exact place and time of your interview. Use a map and familiarise yourself with the location so you don't get lost. *A late arrival is never excusable*. At best you will only antagonise the recruiter and make yourself anxious and nervous – certainly *not* the best way to begin the last phase of your job search!

Remember to bring a copy of your CV or application form with you, as the company may want to see it. They may also want you to fill in an extra form which you won't feel confident completing without the relevant information at your fingertips.

Know your interviewer's name, correct pronunciation and his/her title. Greet the interviewer by his/her surname and shake hands firmly. Remember, now is the time to begin your positive approach. Talk to the interviewer on the way into the interview room. Statements like 'your company was easy to find' or 'what nice modern offices' will ensure you begin to create a good impression. Don't overdo it though. Being over-friendly or sycophantic will definitely *not* win you the job. If the secretary or receptionist greets you and shows you to the interview room, be polite; they may well be asked how you behaved. If you are kept waiting, receive any apologies gracefully and don't make a fuss, however angry and frustrated you may feel. This is not the time to antagonise the interviewer. Memorise the experience as a point of candidate care that you will improve if you join the company; this will help you keep calm and maintain your positive approach.

Before you go into the interview room you may be asked if you would like to leave your coat, bags etc. outside. *Do so*. Taking outdoor wear inside the interview room makes you look like an 'outsider' and you want to create the impression of already being on the 'inside' of the company. Similarly, don't refer to your present employer as 'we'. 'We do our accounts this way.' 'We've manufactured components like this for several years.' Speaking in this way again puts up a barrier between you and the recruiter. So whenever possible talk about your present employer in the third person. 'At ABC Company I . . .'; 'The ABC Company method is to . . .'.

Remember too that the interviewer may be nervous, indeed it could be their first interview as a recruiter! So help them (and yourself) as much as possible. Be polite and assertive, smile as much as you can and look them in the eye. This will help you create a positive impression and so help

you relax. The more relaxed you are at interviews the more confident you will sound.

Selection tests
....

Many employers are now using a variety of questionnaires and tests to supplement the information they get from you at the interview.

These may take on a number of different forms
but all are geared to providing evidence of the
skills that you have talked about at your interview or written on your application form. They
will also be used to help the company decide
whether you really have the necessary background knowledge and experience to do the job.

The first requirement from you as a candidate
is not to panic! While any form of written test
tends to remind us of school exams and all the
misery they may have entailed, recruitment tests
are actually a more objective way of finding out
about you than an interview is. So if, like many
people, you find it difficult to sell yourself at
interviews then the tests and questionnaires the
company uses can often help make up for a less
than confident interview performance.

Tests are administered either before or after the
interview and the company should warn you in
advance as to their nature and the time you will
have to complete them. If not, ask. It is important
to remember that you are not being singled out;
all the candidates for the job will be asked to

complete the same test. Indeed you may find yourself taking a particular test alongside other candidates. Don't be put off by them, but concentrate on your own performance.

Whatever the form, follow the instructions carefully, work methodically through the test and leave yourself time to check your answers at the end. If you are faced with a particular difficult question which you can't answer, leave it and go back to it if there's time at the end. It is better to do yourself justice by answering well those questions you know than by wasting time on those you do not. In some cases, however, you will be asked to complete all the questions provided and you should make sure you time-manage yourself so that you have enough time to complete whatever is asked of you.

If you are applying for a clerical or secretarial job that asks for typing or wordprocessing skills then you can be sure the company will give you an accuracy and/or speed test . . . so brush up on your skills before you go! The same is true for research jobs where you may be asked to undertake a piece of 'on-the-spot' research, or an accountancy post where you could be asked to analyse a set of figures. Think ahead and be prepared for whatever tests you think may be appropriate in your field of work.

In particular, a written component of the interview process may consist of short answers or ticking answer boxes in a multiple-choice questionnaire. If this is the case, the company are probably using one of the widely available psychometric instruments. These are not actual tests, in the real sense of the word, but are a way of discovering what you are like as a person and how you are likely to behave at work. There is no point in lying or second-guessing when completing these questionnaires. Most have a 'lie detector' factor built in and even if you did manage to bluff your way through you may end up with a job more suited to the person you pretended to be in the questionnaire than to you!

Most companies will give you the results of your test or personality questionnaire and may wish to discuss aspects of them with you at the interview. If you don't receive this feedback from them then contact them after the interview to find out how you did; you are entitled to have this information and to be given the opportunity to give your comments on it, but be as constructive as you can rather than saying 'It was unfair.'

Some companies will go further than a single questionnaire or test and invite you to attend for a day with them. In this case they may use a linked series of tests and exercises besides an interview. This linked process is often referred to as an Assessment Centre. All the information gathered on you during the day is compared to the requirements of the job and a decision on your suitability is then based on the performance you have given across all the exercises and tests.

Only those trained in assessment techniques can run these days and the person(s) assessing you will probably also conduct your interview. The key is to be yourself. You may be asked to give a presentation, to complete a written exercise or to take part in a group discussion on a given topic, with other candidates. Don't be tempted to try and outdo the competition. You will be judged on your contribution to any discussion and if you appear overly aggressive you may well be marked down! On the other hand make sure you have your say and, while remaining flexible, be willing to back your arguments and opinions.

In the same way, think about any presentations you may be asked to give. If you have time to prepare before attending an Assessment Centre, then try it out on a friend or relative first. Were they interested in what you had to say? Was your content and your delivery fresh and interesting? If you don't have the opportunity to prepare before the day then during the preparation time you are given, ask yourself the same questions as outlined above. Remember, your clarity, speed of delivery and tonal quality is as important as the content.

Above all, try and remain calm and positive. If you complete one exercise and you are unhappy with your performance don't let it put you off for the rest of the day; it may mean that your strongest exercise is about to come. If you perform well overall then this is most likely to override a weak performance on any individual exercise.

Whether it's a single test, questionnaire or battery of exercises, remember that all of the information being looked at is on or about you! So, if you have done your homework and are aware of your strengths and how you are working on the less developed aspects of yourself, then you have little to worry about. If you don't get the job then do ensure that you get your feedback after the event and use this for subsequent assessments.

Whatever the outcome, the experience will definitely help to prepare you for future tests, questionnaires or assessments of this kind and you can positively build on your experience and learning for future job applications. More and more companies of varying sizes are now moving towards using assessments as well as interviews to select people for jobs and so it is likely you will meet some form of testing at some stage in your job search or subsequent career. None of this, however, negates the importance of a good interview performance and if the interview is the only method of selection, then it almost goes without saying that you cannot afford to present yourself badly. A weak performance at an interview can lose you the job and so it is always worth taking extra time and effort to prepare for the interview itself.

The interview
....

Some sources say that interviews are won or lost in the first 45 seconds. This may or may not be the case, but the message the statement carries is a clear one: *First impressions count and so you must get your interview nerves under control as soon as possible.* Your initial answers will sound more coherent if you have prepared a short résumé of your current position. Initial questions usually concentrate on 'what are you doing now?' or 'tell us something about yourself'. The résumé will help you remember key points you want to make and enable you to highlight your achievements, skills and successes. These are your selling points and so need emphasising as often as possible.

Your task is to sound positive about yourself. Don't admit a weakness without showing the ability to make up for it or a willingness to learn how to change it. Similarly, don't talk about what you *can't* or *won't* do, but about how you see yourself working effectively in the new job. A recruiter is unlikely to take on someone who has listed 101 reasons that convey difficulty about working for their company.

Remember too that a successful interview is a *two-way* process. The employer is trying to determine if you have the necessary qualifications and experience for the job opening. You must determine whether the company will give you the opportunity to achieve your potential growth and development. You'll help this process work if you ask and answer questions clearly and concisely and *listen carefully* to the information the recruiter gives you about the job, taking mental notes.

Who will interview you?

No two firms interview in the same way. At one interview you may find your future manager and a representative from personnel, at another there may be up to five interviewers from various interested departments. Don't panic or be put off by a sea of faces. You are not expected to take them all on at once! No matter how many people are present, in every case the rule remains the same. Each interviewer will ask you about a different aspect of your experience and the vacancy on offer. Once you have been introduced give your full attention and establish eye contact with the person asking the questions, while referring to the other interviewers only if they interject or if a point is particularly important to their area of work. In this way you will maintain your confidence and concentration levels and ensure you give sufficient time and attention to each interviewer and the questions they ask.

Preliminary and subsequent interviews

You may find when you arrive for your interview that it takes the form of a preliminary discussion. At this stage one or two managers will interview you, asking you questions about your background and experience. On the strength of this they will judge your suitability to go forward for a second or final interview. Alternatively you may attend only one interview with more than one interviewer – up to five is rare but not uncommon! The outcome will then depend on your performance at the time. The company will usually tell you what form this and subsequent interviews will take. If they don't and you are asked back for a second or third interview, it is more than permissible to phone the contact point and politely ask who will be present at the next interview.

Questions the interviewer may ask you
....

It is impossible to forecast all the questions you might be asked at an interview and anyway, over-preparing is not a good idea as it can make you sound stilted and unnatural. This is not, however, a good excuse for not doing any preparation at all! Experience has shown that there are a number of interview questions that commonly arise and as part of your research for the vacancy you should anticipate these questions and work out appropriate and effective answers to them. At the interview you don't have to give the exact answers you have previously worked through, but thinking through your strategy beforehand will help you focus your mind on the form the interview will take and the questions you are, therefore, most likely to be asked.

To help you, look at the questions on the next few pages and tailor them to your specific purpose.

Introductory questions

Tell us something about yourself

What is your present position?

What project are you working on at the moment?

These introductory questions are asked to help you settle down while you talk about a subject you know something about – namely you! They are used by the recruiter to find out who you are and what you do and it may also help you to realise that they give the recruiter a chance to relax and make sure they've collected the right candidate!

Your aim should be to give the person interviewing you a well-explained and concise résumé of yourself. Make three points (the interviewer won't be able to absorb more); tell them:

What you are doing now

The nature of your work

Briefly, what you did in your previous position if you aren't currently in full-time paid employment

This is more than enough information for the recruiter to use to ask subsequent questions. It will also act as a positive introduction to you and will give some indication of the framework and structure you work within.

Don't be tempted to give too much information at this stage and remember, the recruiter wants to know about you in a work context, *not* about you and your domestic arrangements, unless they are pertinent to the job.

If you have been on a career break or unemployed for some time you need to think carefully about your answers to these introductory questions. Try and pick up on the positive things you've been doing since leaving paid work. You may wish to focus on any new skills and interests you've acquired or courses you've taken. Above all sound positive about your time away from paid work. You may wish to include in your answer information about your last paid job. It is up to you to decide whether this is relevant or not and depends on the length of time you have been away from paid employment.

Career background

Why are you leaving/did you leave your present/previous job?

Why did you wait so long before thinking of moving from your present/previous job?

Why have you not been able to find another job?

Why did you take a career break?

Why were you selected for redundancy?

Wouldn't you rather work for a larger company?

Would you find it difficult working for a commercial/public company?

These questions will build up a picture of you and why you are seeking change.

Be positive when you talk about leaving your present or previous job. You are looking for a new challenge, promotion, increased training facilities, *not* more money. Also remember to emphasise that you are leaving a job or returning to work after a break, because you want *this* job with *this* company, not just any job.

If you have been in one job for some time emphasise the variety the job has given you and changes that have occurred, especially those you've instigated or implemented.

If you talk about redundancy, ensure you convey the impression that the post and/or department were made redundant and *not* you as an individual. Show that you have been looking for a position like the one the company is offering and are *not* prepared to take just any job.

Emphasis should also be put on the pressures you have worked under and the budgetary limits you have been able to meet. If you are moving from a *large* to a small company it may also be useful to say that the department you have worked for is medium-sized or small even though your company as a whole is vast. This gives the impression that you would have no trouble working with a smaller number of people in a close-knit team.

Personal attributes: your skills, achievements and strengths

> *What do you see as your greatest strength as an employee?*

What have been your best achievements?

What did you enjoy doing most in your last job?

What are the qualities needed in a good secretary/clerk/administrative manager?

What do you feel you gained above all from your last job/your time away from paid employment?

If we offer you a job what are the greatest assets you have to offer us?

In what areas do you feel your expertise lies?

Here is your opportunity to shine! Make positive points about yourself drawn from your work and leisure experiences. If appropriate you can cite actual examples of how and where you've excelled. Your detailed preparation will help you here. You should also take the opportunity to make links between what you have done and the experience and qualities the company is looking for. So if, for example, in the advert the company mentions the ability to write reports and the recruiter asks the question at the interview 'What did you enjoy doing in your last job?' make sure your answer includes reference to how much you enjoy report writing!

If you've never written a report at work but write them all the time for the local youth club or residents' association, then ensure you convey this information to the recruiter. Even though it's work you've undertaken in your leisure time it's still a skill the company is looking for. This is a simple technique to adopt and one that is *very effective* in practice.

Self-perception

How would your present/past employer describe you?

How would you describe yourself?

How would your work colleagues/friends describe you?

What is your working/management style?

These, again, are questions which you need to answer by promoting yourself.

If you find it difficult to talk about your positive qualities in the first person then relate what other people (managers, friends or colleagues) have said about you. Here you should also think about the type of person the company has stated they are looking for and, within reason, match your 'best' qualities to their person specification.

Your weaknesses

What do you enjoy doing least at work?

What things did you find most difficult in your last job?

What areas would you feel least confident in if we offered you the job?

What training do you feel you will need if you join us?

How has your time away from work affected you?

Why should we consider you with your lack of experience in 'X'?

Do you feel your skills are too specialised for us?

The first thing to remember is that everyone has weaknesses and while you may not have much experience of 'X' the other candidates may know very little about 'Y', your strongest attribute.

The rules for admitting a weakness are:

1 Ensure it's not a key requirement of the job.

2 Immediately back up what action you are taking/have taken to turn your weakness into a strength. For example, you could say 'My knowledge of French is rusty so I'm taking an evening course to improve it.'

If you are criticised for knowing too much or too little about a subject balance the situation by explaining what you do know, how other named strengths you have will help you or how you could help train others, given your experience in a particular area.

These answers will impress recruiters as they will see they have before them a candidate who knows him or herself and can see *where* and *how* they can benefit the organisation.

Your temperament

If people gossiped about you behind your back, what would they be saying?

If faced with problem 'A' how would you handle it?

Have you ever faced problem 'B'? How did you solve it?

Are you a team member or a loner?

Would working in a cramped office upset you?

What makes you laugh?

What makes you angry?

These questions are asked in order to determine whether you'll fit into the company. Here again your preparation will help you. Be honest about yourself but don't be negative. 'I *won't* work in a cramped office' could just lose you the job. 'I'd rather not, but I'd make the most of it' will encourage the recruiter to see you as a positive person prepared to make the best of a bad situation.

Think what the company is looking for as you shape your answers – is it looking for a team player or someone to work alone? You should also ask yourself whether *you* will be happy with the arrangements the recruiter is telling you about.

Your research and perception of the job

How does this job fit in with your long-term career plans?

What do you think you'll be doing in three years' time?

Why do you think you are the best person for the job?

What can you contribute to this company?

Why should we offer you the job?

What did you do to prepare for this interview?

What do you know about this company?

How would your experience be put to best use here?

These are the key questions asked by recruiters to find out what you are going to offer the company and just how much you have tried to find out about them.

Concentrate on your *best qualities* when answering. Where appropriate – and especially if you find it difficult to talk positively about yourself – give examples of how your previous experience will be put to good use within the company. This is also the time to remind the recruiter of your *unique selling point* – you want to be remembered as a strong candidate with positive attributes to offer when the recruiter reviews this part of the interview. It is also important to give the recruiter the impression that, if feasible, you wish to stay with the company and take advantage of career and training opportunities. Unless a short-term contract is being offered, no recruiter is going to employ and spend money on training someone who they feel will only stay in the job for a short time.

Why do you want the job?

Why do you want to join this company?

How do you feel you would fit in here?

What important things do you look for in a job?

It is surprising how many candidates cannot answer the question 'Why do you want this job?' Yet it is the one above all others that requires a well-thought-out answer. Tailor your answer to the criteria the company has given you and if the question is asked in the abstract, i.e. 'What is your ideal job?', make sure you answer by describing the job on offer!

Your arrangements

How far will you have to travel daily if you join us?

The company will be moving to 'X' next year, will this be a problem for you?

How would you feel being away from home five nights a month?

What were your earnings in your last job?

Is the salary level important to you?

Will your career break affect your future working arrangements?

When the recruiter begins to ask specific questions such as these you know you are coming to the end of the interview, but you must *continue* to present a positive image.

Use this opportunity to reassure the recruiter that travelling long distances, attending training programmes etc. present no problems to you.

Don't say 'No, I won't move', 'I won't travel', etc. If this is the case, wait until you are offered the job: that is *your time* to negotiate. The same is true for the question 'Will your career break affect your future working arrangements?' If you have taken a career break to have a baby or raise a child this question may be used to find out about your child-care arrangements. Again, it's important to present a positive picture and assure the recruiter that all necessary provisions have been made and that your work patterns will not be affected. Remember the time to negotiate is *after you've been offered the job*.

Your questions
Is there anything you would like to ask me/us at this stage?

All properly conducted interviews should give you a chance to ask questions at the end. If no opportunity is given and you do have questions, ask at the end of the interview when would be a convenient time to raise them.

At this stage don't feel you must ask questions if you have none. A simple 'no questions at the moment thank you, we seem to have covered the main points' will suffice. If you are going to ask questions don't enquire about salary, vacation, bonuses or benefits. Your aim is to show how you can benefit the company by what you have

to offer. The time for meeting *your* own requirements is at the negotiation stage. If really pressed
for an answer on salary, indicate first that you
are more interested in the opportunities the company has to offer and then name a salary *range*.
This technique will leave you and the recruiter
room for negotiation without causing embarrassment.

This is, however, your opportunity to leave the
recruiter with a really strong impression of your
candidature. If you can, end the interview on a
positive statement about you rather than on a
question. You can re-emphasise a piece of information given during the interview, for example:
'I don't have any questions at the moment but I
just want to say I am really interested in the
training and development project you mentioned
and that my experience in administrative co-
ordination will be of help with it.' Or, give a new
piece of information that might have been missed
during the interview. For example, 'We haven't
talked about my job with ATD Insurance at all,
and while I was there I had 18 months' experience in accounts which I think might be useful in
this job.' Your positive concluding statement will
be remembered long after the questions are for-
gotten.

Finally

....

1 Make sure you don't criticise your previous
employer however much you feel like doing so!

....

This really should be avoided as much as possible. The interview should be kept positive at all times. If you *really* feel you must be negative about your employer, then prepare how you do it and ensure you show how *you* have made the best of a bad situation.

2 If you find you are arguing with the recruiter, make your points firmly and politely and leave yourself room to back out of a confrontation, so that you can both save face. The aim is to be assertive *not* aggressive.

3 At the end of the interview it is possible that you won't have had the opportunity to give the recruiter a vital piece of information about yourself, which could help you win the job. If this is the case, include this information when you are given your chance to ask questions.

4 If you know you are waffling or answering a question badly, have the confidence to stop. State that you're not answering well, and go back to the beginning. The recruiter will respect you for taking this course of action and you won't miss out on answering what could be an important question.

The same technique holds for technical questions. If you can't answer say you don't know but that you would consult such and such a textbook to find the answer. The recruiter will move on to another question which you should find you *can* answer.

5 If at any time you don't understand the recruiter's question ask them to clarify; you *don't* want to answer the wrong question at the wrong time!

End the interview on a positive note. Thank the interviewer(s) for their time, shake hands if appropriate and make sure you know the correct way out of the room. Candidates have lost the chance of a job offer by walking into a cupboard instead of out of the door!

Positive and negative factors evaluated by a recruiter

During the course of the interview the recruiter will be evaluating positive as well as negative factors about you. Listed here are the negative and positive factors frequently evaluated and the reason these are often instrumental in leading to the hiring or rejection of a candidate.

Negative factors

Factor	*Response*
Unsatisfactory personal appearance/ inappropriate dress.	Would not represent the company in a positive way; unprofessional in front of visitors and clients.
Boasting as opposed to selling yourself. Presenting unwanted reports and documents.	Big-headed, egocentric and unable to follow directions.

Late/unprepared for interview. Unable to find way out.	Would not be organised/dependable on the job.
Overaggressive/ defensive/arrogant/ sullen attitude/ swearing.	Would be 'difficult' to work with and would not get along with other employees.
Inability to express thoughts or questions clearly.	Unsatisfactory verbal skills, unable to think or express ideas coherently.
Lack of interest and enthusiasm, especially when considering future goals.	Passive, no initiative, no imagination, no clear purpose.
Evasiveness.	Unwilling to take personal responsibility, will make excuses and blame others for mistakes. May well be hiding something.
Talking at length about domestic situation.	Immature, indiscreet, will bring personal problems into the office.
Criticising/condemning past or present employer.	The recruiter will feel you are being negative and that you will criticise their company if they give you the job.

Failure to look interviewer in the eye, weak handshake, nervous behaviour.	Lack of confidence or hiding something.

Positive factors

Factor	*Response*
Being on time and knowing where to go. Having with you all necessary documentation.	Organised and professional.
Smiling, sitting comfortably, looking recruiter in the eye.	Relaxed and positive, Able to function well under pressure.
Making *occasional* joke or amusing remark.	Confident, not afraid to present lighter side of personality.
Giving clear information on the company and the position.	Candidate taken opportunity to research company, will be thorough if given the job.
Talking positively about yourself and your achievements.	Able to present candidature positively and confidently.
Making suggestions for tackling the job if it were offered to you.	Ability to initiate and innovate, having undertaken research.

Giving examples of how you made a success of your last job and offering one or two ideas for the new job.	Will bring same success to new company and job.
Not giving in under pressured questioning. Remaining assertive.	Clear, concise thinker, able to present ideas logically when under pressure.
Asking intelligent questions about the position without going over the points already covered during interview.	Good research of position, able to deal positively with situation.
Showing clear career direction within the company.	Well motivated and ambitious. Thoughtful.

Keep a copy of these *positive interview factors* with your application form or CV and read through them before you go into the interview room. You will then be fully prepared to give the most positive impression of your candidature.

If the interview has gone well, towards the end you may become aware of behaviour by the recruiter which suggests they may intend to shortlist you or even offer you the job. This behaviour could include:

Leaning forward

Longer eye contact

Discussion about holidays, pay, hours, etc.

Questions about the practicalities of employment, for example asking when can you start

The recruiter looking more relaxed

If you detect any of this behaviour it should enhance your overall presentation and confidence level. It does not mean, however, that you have definitely got the job, so *do not* become blasé and lose what could be *your* new position. Remember, to achieve *interview success* you must work hard and concentrate on your interview from the moment you enter the building.

After the interview

Reviewing your performance

It is important to review your performance after each interview. The Review Chart will help you do this clearly and concisely. If the interview went well it will highlight the positive points you made, which you will want to remember and repeat next time. If the session was disappointing it will help you identify the areas and questions where you felt least confident. Once you have identified these you can build on the experience and ensure your performance is improved for subsequent interviews.

The Review Chart will also provide you with the detail you need if you are going to write a follow-up letter.

Review chart

Date of interview:
Company:
Interviewed by:
Title(s):

1 What I did well

2 Important successes/achievements I highlighted including my unique selling point

3 Good answers I gave

4 Poor answers I gave

5 Areas of questioning where I felt uncomfortable and unprepared

6 Things I will do differently next time

7 Any other points about this interview which are important and which will be helpful for subsequent interviews

Try to complete a review chart after each interview. The sooner you do this the better you will remember the answers you gave. Given time you can remember in a different light, or even forget completely the poor answers you gave! Yet these are the very points that need to be remembered and improved on for next time.

Follow-up action

If you are interested in the job it will benefit your application if you write a brief follow-up letter the next day. This should thank the interviewer(s) for their time and reaffirm your interest. This letter will be added to the information the interviewer(s) already have on you and so will enhance the positive impression you have created.

Sample letter

                                              Your name
                                              Your address
Your telephone no.
(day and evening)   Date

The interviewer and company name
address

Dear Mr, Ms, Miss –

    First paragraph   Thank the recruiter for the interview in respect of the position of . . . . Also include any reference numbers from the original advertisement.

    Second paragraph   Reaffirm your interest in the job.

    Third paragraph   Indicate once more that you appreciate being considered and are available for interview if other managers wish to see you.
Yours sincerely

YOUR SIGNATURE
Your name printed.

If you are not successful after an interview you *must* build on the experience for the future.

1 Investigate (by contacting the company recruiter and from your own review) why you didn't get the job and formulate plans to improve your performance next time.

2 If you would still like to work for the company and the interview you had was positive, you could consider writing a holding letter. This thanks the recruiter for the interview and tells them you are still interested in their company and would like your name to be kept on file. If they felt you were a good candidate they may well call you back for interview if a similar vacancy arises. Remember, while job hunting it pays to be *politely persistent*.

The following is an example of the type of holding letter you could write.

> Your name
> Your address
> Date

The company's name and address

Dear (*named person*)

   Thank you for your recent letter advising me that I have not been selected for the post of . . . . reference . . . . . . at my recent interview.

. . . .

I understand that you were looking for someone with more . . . . experience and hope that you were able to make an appointment for the post.

I wish you to know that I am still very interested in working for : . . . . At my interview we discussed my background in . . . ./training as . . . . and I wonder if you are anticipating any vacancies in this area/these areas/at your . . . . branch. If so, I should very much like to be considered.

Would it be possible for you to retain my CV or could you let me know when you will next be advertising?

With many thanks for your advice in this matter and for seeing me at the recent interview. I look forward to hearing from you.

Yours sincerely

YOUR SIGNATURE
Your name printed.

Assessing the job offer

If you are selected by the company to fill the vacancy, you will receive an offer of employment. Use the following checklist to help you decide whether to accept the job. The job search is a two-way process and you must ensure you are going to be happy in the new job and are satisfied with the conditions of employment before accepting the company's offer. If the job is not right for you and you accept it, you will soon begin to feel disillusioned and depressed. This can affect your confidence level and result in poor job performance, which will be unacceptable to you and your new employer. So think very carefully before accepting a job offer, especially if it is the first one you are offered after a period away from paid work. You may be tempted to take any job to get back into full-time employment, but many job searchers say that taking the first job that 'came along' was a mistake and resulted in a further job-searching exercise which left them feeling demoralised. Remember, if you have been successful at interview once you will be again, and the right job may well come from a subsequent interview.

Job offer – checklist
Award points out of 10 for the following and asterix (*) your three most important needs.

Needs	Points
Salary	–
Benefits	–
Prospects for training and promotion	–
Interesting work	–
Friendly environment	–
Convenient location and suitable hours	–

Results

46+   This job, as presented to you, meets your needs and looks promising. Before you accept the position make sure the company's terms and conditions of employment match your expectations.

30–46   The job is of some interest to you. Is it possible to talk to the company's representative and renegotiate those aspects which you gave low marks? This is particularly important if they are the categories marked*. How long will you have to accept the aspects of the job that don't satisfy you? If it is only for a relatively short time then it may be worth accepting the job for the longer-term rewards and experience it will give you.

Below 30   It does not appear that this job meets your own needs. Do you have all the necessary and correct information about the job? If you have, it may be best to refuse the job offer and use the experience as a good indication of how to achieve interview success to secure the right job.

When assessing the offer, concentrate particularly on the areas you might want to develop for the future. A job might hold your interest for six months to a year while you are still in the learning phase but what are the prospects for you after that? If you are an executive secretary or administrator, will the company offer you training prospects on new office equipment, or the opportunity to progress into a full management position once you have proved yourself in your first job? The complaint most often voiced by job seekers is that a job was 'sold' to them as having more responsibility than was actually the case. So beware of titles such as 'Company Administrations Executive', 'Executive Personnel Co-ordinator' and the like – they may well be masking glorified clerical positions, when your aim has been to make a first or second management move.

The same is true if you are entering a profession with a recognised training programme, for example nursing, the law or banking. Will the institution you train with promote you once you are qualified or will you have to move location on completion of your training? This is particularly important if you are a late entrant into a profession, with domestic or financial ties which prevent you from moving around the country in order to further your career.

In each instance the procedure remains the same: before you accept the offer investigate *all* aspects of the company and the job as fully as you possibly can. No recruiter will mind you asking questions at this stage because they are keen for you to fill their vacancy. If there is something that you're not happy about then now is also the time to negotiate. A company is unlikely to double your salary (unless you have exceptional skills and negotiating powers!) but if you are incurring additional expenses it might be prepared to offer £500–£1000 more, depending on the nature of the vacancy, or promise you an early salary review date.

So, if you are unhappy with an aspect of a job offer and as long as you are prepared to compromise, it is worth negotiating with a prospective employer to enhance the terms of employment offered to you. But do try to be flexible. If you make too many demands you may end up losing the offer altogether, so think very carefully before contacting the company and make sure you leave yourself and the recruiter room to manoeuvre. If the company meets your request then you can accept the offer knowing you have positively helped your position. If the company won't meet your demand (or agree a compromise with you) at least you will have tried and can now assess whether to take the job as originally offered.

5

....

Speculative approaches and

the hidden job market

In addition to applying formally for jobs, through advertisements in magazines, newspapers and through recruitment agencies, it is important to expand your network of contacts and seek informal help from every quarter. You should let not only your friends and relatives but also your work contacts and past acquaintances know you are job searching, and ask them to talk to people on your behalf. If you are hoping to gain promotion within your present company then you must also make sure your managers, and the managers of the department you wish to join, know who you are and what you can do.

If you have had a career break or are redundant (and can bear the thought of working for the same company as your partner!) then ask your partner to talk to his or her colleagues and contacts about you.

This method of job searching is known as *networking*. In practice it is the process of making and developing relationships which can help lead to a job offer. There is nothing manipulative or underhand about this as a method of job searching. It is, in fact, widely used in business and is simply another avenue of research you should develop in your quest for the right job for you.

It is valuable because other people can help you to research your potential job market in more depth, suggest additional information that you should research (often from sources you wouldn't have thought of), offer you ideas and share experiences. You, in turn, will be able to offer them help, either now or in the future, and that becomes a real strength because the whole underlying philosophy of networking is that it is mutually beneficial.

Talking about your ambitions and experience in this way, to as wide a group of people as possible, may well lead to avenues of opportunity that you had not previously considered.

Adding to the strength of the networking route is the following statistic, which applies whether you are looking for in-company promotion or a job with a new company.

Performance at interview or in your present job counts for 10 per cent of your job search. Another 30 per cent is based on the *image* you project, either at work, if you are looking for a new job within your present company, or at your interview when dealing with a potential new employer. That leaves 60 per cent, and that 60 per cent is based on *exposure*. How well known are you? Have you seen round a new company or department and talked to its managers about their new product or pay scheme? Have you attended their open day and spoken to as many people as possible? Wherever you are job searching the rule remains the same: *the better known you are the better chance you have of securing the job you want.*

Making Contacts

The first stage in your networking campaign is to compile a list of likely contacts who can help and advise you. Think as broadly as you possibly can and then enter names, addresses and phone numbers onto an index with a note of when you last contacted them. You may find the pages at the end of this book will help you set this up.

The following suggestions should help you begin your Contact List and do remember to add additional names and contact points each time you meet or speak to someone new.

Contacts

Home and personal

Family

Friends

Neighbours

Personal banker

Insurance broker

Hairdresser

Accountant

Old school teachers/lecturers/tutors

Work

Colleagues

Retired colleagues

Personnel department

Current customers and suppliers

Other work contacts

People in related organisations

People you have met at trade fairs etc.

Social

Voluntary organisation members

Clubs or society members

Members of religious community

Remember, none of these people will necessarily have jobs to offer you but all of them may know of someone who does!

Speculative approaches

Making yourself known to outside companies is also important when considering potential vacancies. Many vacant jobs are never advertised. They are filled by someone, like yourself, writing a speculative letter or making a telephone call to a company to see whether it has a suitable opening. The most positive result of this is that sometimes an employer creates a vacancy for the right candidate, so that you could find yourself being interviewed alone without competition, before a vacancy arises or a job is advertised. Even if the company doesn't go as far as to create a vacancy for you it may well interview you for a post it has already advertised, or interview you ahead of the field for a job it had anticipated advertising. Remember, if you get a job in this way you will already have saved your new company the cost of advertising and recruiting!

The advantage of speculative approaches is that it demonstrates your initiative to an employer, who in turn is likely to be impressed that you want to know more about the company and employment opportunities within it. The disadvantage is that you may well find yourself writing a great number of letters, thus drawing considerably on your own time and resources. You must be careful to achieve the right balance between a realistically researched approach and a speculative waste of time. For example, don't write to a company that has recently announced redundancies or falling profits. Instead you should begin by writing to companies you think will be most likely to have openings for someone with your qualifications and experience. Find out from public libraries or the company itself the name of an individual to write to. The *Kompass Directory*, kept by your public library, is another excellent source of company information which also gives geographical locations.

Keep your letters short, typed if possible, and to the point. The example letters from Chapter 3 will help you.

Telephone contact

If you have said in your letter that you will phone the company in six days' time to arrange a meeting you *must* do just that. If you didn't say you would phone but haven't heard from the company after ten days then you should phone by way of a gentle reminder!

Before phoning make sure you know to whom you need to speak and what you are going to say. Write down in advance the points you wish to make and practise speaking out loud. If you are on your own this is particularly important. Few things sound stranger than hearing your own voice on the phone if you haven't spoken all day!

The company contact you speak to is probably busy with other work and while you are geared up to talk about yourself they may not know who you are or what you want. Obviously, this initial introduction is easier if you know the individual concerned or have been recommended to them but, whichever is the case, introduce yourself clearly and slowly, telling the contact why you are phoning and then leaving them space to talk. Listen carefully to what they say and have a pen and paper with you to write down any instructions they give you. Repeat back dates, addresses and times of appointments to make sure you have them right. It pays to be politely persistent; if they can't see you, ask them if there is someone else you can speak to or information they can send you. Try not to take *no* for an answer, but don't be rude or aggressive and never swear even if your frustration has reached boiling point! If it helps you, stand rather than sit when talking on the phone; this will help you maintain a *positive* frame of mind. If the firm will not see you, it is simply because they do not have the time. *Do not* take it as a personal reflection on you. They may, however, keep your CV and contact you when a suitable vacancy arises.

The speculative meeting
If the contact does see you the ball is firmly in your court. There are four possible outcomes:

1 You may be told that while there are no vacancies at present your CV will be retained by the company and you should apply formally when they next advertise.

2 There are a number of openings shortly to be advertised and the company will see you for a formal interview.

3 They will interview you for an unadvertised vacancy as soon as possible.

4 They will recommend someone else for you to talk to.

The rule of a speculative 'information meeting' of this kind is to ensure that you and your potential contact or employer do not lose face over the situation.

It is essential, therefore, that you take control at the outset showing interest, an enquiring attitude, listening and being forthcoming when invited. Treat the discussion as an exploratory first interview. Remember, if you are seen by a company contact you may be invited back for a formal interview and should leave a good impression which you can build on next time. In this case, therefore, find out all you can about the company before you meet the person you contacted. The more *informed* interest you can show the more likely you are to be considered for future vacancies.

The person you see will, no doubt, ask you questions about your skills and experience based on your CV, so ensure you prepare for these thoroughly and don't forget to read Chapter 4 of this book – Interview Success – before you meet your prospective employer!

Planning an Information Meeting

Given that you need to put some thought into your information meeting before you go, the following may be of some help to you.

As ever, good presentation is essential. Think through very carefully what your purpose is in going to see each person you have contacted. Be certain about what you want to accomplish in the meeting and the specific information you wish to gain. Draw up a list of questions which are appropriate for that person and draw up for yourself an informal agenda which should include:

1 Introductions

You need to begin by 'breaking the ice' probably by chatting about shared experience, acknowledging shared achievements and social contacts, or if the individual is a contact made through your own speculative approach or is someone who you did not previously know, simply by thanking them for seeing you.

2 Why you requested the meeting

At this point make sure your contact understands that you intend to keep the meeting brief and that you don't expect them to offer you a job. Do this by positively explaining why you are there and what you are trying to achieve, e.g. other contacts, more information, or an idea of future vacancies in a particular area, etc.

3 Information

As appropriate, now is the time to move on to discuss your options. Can this contact advise you on job exploration and experience required? Do they know how companies in your chosen area of work undertake recruitment and do they, for example, use Assessment Centres? What is the current state of the businesses in this area and what successful companies do they know of or have they been involved with?

4 Your ideas

These are particularly important if you are meeting with a potential employer. Having tried them out elsewhere first, be prepared to talk about the innovative ideas you have for the area of work. If they are concise, practical and in tune with the thinking of your contact, they will create a positive impression of you and your work style.

5 Advice

It may be appropriate to ask them for advice on your CV and your general presentation. If the contact knows you well it might also be worth asking what they see as your main strengths and weaknesses – make sure you're not over persistent on personal areas, however, as you don't want your contact to get embarrassed or enter into a heated discussion on your worst faults!

6 Objectives

Check out with your contact whether they think your objectives for your job search and future career are realistic – if they are hesitant, it's worth asking what other areas they think are worth exploring.

7 Ending the meeting

As always, thank them for their time and, if possible, leave them a copy of your CV. If they recommend other people to contact then make sure you establish whether you or they are going to approach the person first – and don't leave without the contact details you need. It may also be possible to ask if you can meet with them to review progress after a suitable period of time. Keep a note of when such a meeting might be appropriate and then ensure you phone or write to the individual nearer the time.

This scenario applies whether you are meeting an old family friend or a potential employer through your own research or through one of your other contacts. The less well known the person is to you, obviously the more formal the meeting will become. You should, therefore, prepare appropriately while following the outline above.

Outcome
....

If the contact was someone you knew well you will most likely go away with some useful information and further contacts. If, additionally, this was a meeting with a potential employer they may feel that they have met someone they regard as a prospective employee for their company.

For your part:

1 You will be considered for future vacancies with the company, or have the names of additional contacts.

2 You will have learnt a great deal about an individual organisation or area of work, which will stand you in good stead for future interviews.

3 You will know when and where vacancies are likely to be advertised.

4 You can be reasonably confident that your CV will be passed around to other contacts.

By taking control of the discussion and showing interest, you will have enhanced your reputation without asking the million-dollar question, 'Can you offer me a job?', which can cause embarrassment on both sides.

As soon as possible after the meeting, it is sensible to write a letter of thanks to the person you have seen. The letter should summarise the points you discussed and confirm any action plans. Again, use the examples on letter writing from Chapter 3 to help you.

Writing this letter is confirmation of the points you should have raised at your discussion:

1 a declared interest in the company and/or the additional information given to you by the contact

2 another name to add to your list of contacts

Make sure you keep all your options open and don't hesitate to write to other individuals and companies and pursue further contacts with them. A second interviewer, for example, may well refer you to a manager in a sister company or someone else within the industry. In this way you will develop your *networking* process, all the time building your knowledge of the industry as a whole, your range of contacts and, above all, the growing possibility of *finding the right job*.

The approach

While the speculative approach can achieve the best results, it can also prove the most disappointing.

Often you will find the person you have contacted cannot see you. Even if you are given the chance of a meeting, it is unlikely to result in an immediate job offer. The best way to prepare for these eventualities is to be realistic.

The approach is geared to increasing your knowledge and extending your list of contacts. It will take some time, perhaps weeks or months, before your contacts will present you with a firm job offer or formal interview, so be prepared for several preliminary discussions at which *you* must always provide the interest and enthusiasm.

Never go to one of these meetings expecting to be offered a job; the chances are you won't be, and you mustn't let unfulfilled expectation lead to increased frustration and disappointment. Secondly, don't be too 'pushy'. Treat the meeting as an exchange of information; if you over-emphasise your wish to be offered a job you may embarrass and lose a potentially helpful contact. If approached correctly, you will find your contact network useful and, ultimately, rewarding.

6

Your new job

Starting a new job is an exciting and challenging prospect but in the first few weeks it can also be quite overwhelming. You will want to make the transition period as stress-free as possible, especially if you have been away from paid work for some time, or have been with your previous employer for many years.

What can you expect? Will your colleagues, staff and managers be helpful and encouraging and will you be able to cope with the office routines and technology? The answer to these questions is *yes*, providing you do your homework and take your time. If you expect miracles on day one you will end up being disappointed!

Before day one

Find out as much as you can about the company before you start your new job. If possible visit your new office and have lunch with your prospective colleagues. If you are taking on a management role you may find your senior managers are already arranging this for you. The more you know about the company and its working practices on your first day the less of a newcomer you will appear. This, in turn, will increase your confidence level.

You must use your initiative and be prepared to work hard to be accepted. If, for example, you find the office word-processing or computer system is different from the one you are used to, ask to be put on a familiarisation course as soon as possible. There's always a great deal to be learnt at the beginning of a new job and the more homework you do beforehand the quicker you will settle in. Your aim is to become an established member of staff as quickly as possible, so make sure you attend as many company induction programmes and meet as many people as you can, right at the start.

Day one and beyond
....

The following 12-point checklist will help you through your first weeks in your new job. We don't suggest you pin it on your wall (!) but it is a good idea to keep it with you as a gentle reminder of the best way to approach your new position.

1 Be on time!

Being late in your first weeks, even by a few minutes, creates a poor and irresponsible impression of you in the minds of other employees.

2 Always carry a *personal notebook*, or diary, and a pen with you.

As you are introduced, write down the names of your new colleagues and other employees/ departments with whom you will be working. In addition make notes about important departmental information and policies. As you add new information this will become an inval- uable reference book for you. *Don't lose it!*

3 Don't assume you can use your colleagues' and manager's first names.

You may have worked for an informal organisation where most employees used each others' first names. The same may not be true of your new company and you should always ask people how they prefer to be addressed. This is also true for people who have 'nicknames'. They may not mind being called by such names by those they've known for years but it may not endear you to them in your first weeks.

If you are a manager coming from a formal organisation where you were called Mr –, Miss –, Mrs –, Ms –, or 'Sir' or 'Madam' and your new company uses first names, you will need to get used to this as soon as possible. *Don't* make yourself unnecessarily unpopular early on, by insisting on your new staff and colleagues adopting working practices from your old company.

4 Measure up the office atmosphere before making changes.

During your first few days, take mental notes regarding the way people act and dress, unwritten office procedures (such as who makes the coffee and the length of lunch breaks) and the general atmosphere in your new office/department. If there's a procedure you don't like, make sure you know why it's done and how others feel about it, before *you* try and change it.

5 Always ask questions when something is unclear – as you are being trained, write down key learning points in your personal notebook or diary.

There is *no* shame in asking for the demonstration of a procedure or added clarification of policy instructions. Any questions you leave unanswered in the initial stages may turn into mistakes when you are on your own. As a manager your staff will respect you for asking them and your colleagues and managers will be willing to help you in your first weeks.

6 For small problems have your manager, colleagues or established member of staff suggest a specific person to help you.

Remember, once you've met them, write their name, job title and phone extension in your book for future reference.

7 Never complain about your job to your staff or colleagues.

Complaining is never a good policy – you never know who might overhear you and *literally* take you up on a chance remark; 'I'm sick of this place', 'I'm leaving' . . . 'I hate so-and-so', etc. Complaining is especially ill-advised when you're new; you will immediately be judged as a person who looks for faults in jobs and people and you will give yourself a bad reputation.

8 Avoid discontented colleagues' complaints and gossip.

Change a negative conversation into a positive one by asking for advice on departmental policy.
Listening to someone else's complaints/ gossip will heighten your own awareness of minor or imagined issues. It is essential for you to remain positive!

9 What to do if you are handed several assignments at once.

Ask for the deadline of each assignment, then prioritise.
If you are in the middle of an assignment for one manager and another gives you an 'urgent' assignment, ask the first manager if theirs can wait. If *not*, have the managers work it out between themselves; it is their problem as well as yours.

10 Learn about overall organisational activities.

If you understand how your job links to others and how your department fits into the company's overall structure, you will not only work more intelligently, but will also find you become valued for your understanding. People who know only their own responsibilities and nothing else – go nowhere.

11 Realise that every job has some duties that are boring.

Just accept them. Once you become established, you can discuss them with your manager and senior colleagues and determine whether or not they are rightfully your responsibility.

12 Don't rush to decorate your work area.

You could alienate yourself by sticking up your favourite posters and surrounding your desk with executive toys or teddy bears! Observe how others in

the company, at your
level, organise their
desk and surrounding
area and, at least
initially, curb your
more outrageous
tendencies!

Above all, be receptive. Listen to what other people have to say and take time to learn the duties and intricacies of your job and department before making changes. This is especially true if you are a new manager. Staff resent a new person coming in and changing their established routines from day one.

Take time to listen to their opinions and make changes slowly and surely, consulting your staff each time you introduce a new procedure or change an existing one. In this way you will establish a good working relationship which will make the transition period that much smoother for all concerned. Remember, *the sooner you get to know the people, the job and the surroundings the more rewarding your new job will be.*

What if it doesn't work out?

All new jobs bring with them bad experiences. You may not find you have the responsibility you hoped for or you might have a particularly difficult manager or member of staff to deal with.

Whatever the problem, give it quiet consideration and above all *time*, to pass over. What looks like a major problem in week one may become negligible by the end of month one, when you will have established allies amongst your staff and colleagues who can help you over the rough patches.

If after a few months there are still major problems you should go and talk them over with personnel, your manager or the head of your department. Normally a talk of this kind will clear the air and adjustments will be made in your working practices. If you get no results from this, however, and you still feel unsatisfied and frustrated you will have to think of leaving. There are two rules to follow in this situation.

1 Try and wait at least nine months before moving jobs again or you may have trouble explaining to a prospective employer why you only stayed a short time. This is especially important if you have no long periods of employment recorded on your CV. You don't want to get a reputation for being a difficult employee or a drifter.

2 However much short-term satisfaction it may give you don't resign on the spot and storm out of the office! You probably need your salary and you should look for work from a position of strength, i.e. with the security of a job behind you. It will help you and creates a much better impression for potential

employers. The message is clear: *even if you hate the job and the company sit tight until you find a new one.*

You will have to put the event down to experience and evaluate what you will do differently next time. Ask yourself whether you rushed into the first job you were offered without thinking through what was really on offer? Were you misled by the recruiter at the time of the interview and promised responsibility that never came to light and did you do your *homework* on the company before taking the position offered? Whatever the reason for your disappointment, build on your experience so that the next job you take is the *right job* for you.

7

....

Useful contacts and

additional reading

There are several agencies and many reference books available to help you with your job search. Your local library will have further details in their reference section, but the following list should provide a good starting point.

Space has been left for you at the end of this section to add your own references and contacts. Write your contact names in as soon as you get them and keep a note of the date so that you'll know when you need to write or phone them again.

Agencies

....

Employment Department
The Employment Department produces booklets on redundancy which can be obtained from Employment Service Jobcentres. Their local office number can be found in the phone book or you can obtain it from your local Citizens Advice Bureau (CAB).

....

Citizens Advice Bureau (CAB)

CAB can give free, independent and confidential advice and information on your employment rights. They also carry leaflets on unemployment and training opportunities and will offer advice on all financial, housing, redundancy and legal matters. Most towns have a CAB and you can find them listed in your local phone book or *Yellow Pages*.

Employment Training

Training and Enterprise Councils (TECs) (England and Wales)

Local Enterprise Companies (LECs) (Scotland)

Northern Ireland Training and Employment Agency
All of these are locally based organisations responsible for ensuring that vocational training relevant to local employment is available. They also encourage the development of local business. They provide information on adult education and vocational guidance and training, together with guidance on starting up in business or becoming self-employed. Again, they are listed in your local phone book or you can ask about them at your local Jobcentre or CAB.

Jobcentres

If you cannot locate your Jobcentre then contact: The Employment Service Head Office on 071 839 5600.

Discrimination

If you think you have been discriminated against at an interview you should first refer the matter to the Managing Director of the company that interviewed you, keeping a record of any letter or telephone calls that pass between you. If you are not satisfied then contact one of the following.

Equal Opportunities Commission, if you feel you have been discriminated against on the grounds of sex or race. Their address is:

Overseas House, Quay Street, Manchester M3 3HN
Tel: 061 833 9244

If you think you have been discriminated against on the grounds of race then contact the Commission for Racial Equality at:

Elliot House, 10–12 Allington Street
London SW1E 5EH
Tel: 071 828 7022

If you think you have been discriminated against for political or religious reasons, in Northern Ireland, write or telephone:

Fair Employment Commission, Andras House
609 Great Victoria Street, Belfast BT2 7BB
Tel: 0232 240020

Further Education and Training

Contact your local TECs, LECs or Northern Ireland Training and Employment Agency – they will have information on vocational training (National Vocational Qualifications and their

Scottish equivalent), and further education opportunities. They can also advise you on grants and loans to help you complete any further training or education you need to undertake.

You can also get in touch with:

Open University, Central Enquiry Service
P.O. Box 71, Milton Keynes MK7 6AG
Tel: 0908 274066

Open College, St Paul's, 781 Wilmslow Road
Didsbury, Manchester M20 8RW
Tel: 061 434 0007

They run a number of vocational and further education courses and can also advise you on how to obtain funding for their programmes.

Counselling Support
If you need counselling either before you begin your job search or to support you through it, you should try:

British Association for Counselling
1 Regent Place, Rugby, Warwicks CV21 2PJ
Tel: 0788 578328

If you are redundant, your employer may also be providing a counselling service or have the name/number of an organisation for you to contact. Your doctor or local health centre will also be able to advise you on the counselling service offered in your area.

If your job search is affecting your relationship:

Relate (who used to be called the Marriage Guidance Council) can be reached via their head office:

Herbert Gray College, Little Church Street
Rugby, Warwicks CV21 3AP
Tel: 0788 573241

Reference Books
••••••••••••••••••••••••••••

Kompass Register of British Industry and Commerce
or *Kompass Directory*
This lists information on over 28,000 companies, most with over 50 employees. It is particularly useful for identifying companies in a given geographical location.

Publisher: Kompass (published annually).

The Times 1000
An annual review of the top 1000 UK companies.

Publisher: Times Books (published annually).

Yellow Pages and Local Directories
Useful for classified local searches.

Floodlight
Information on London-based day and evening classes. Courses include creative writing, self-presentation, interpersonal skills and assertiveness

as well as work-based skills, vocational and further education programmes.

To find out about regional classes across the UK, contact your local TEC, LEC or local education authority.

General Reading
••••••••••••••••••••••••••••••

There are many books and pamphlets available on career change, interviews, becoming self-employed, assertiveness and self-presentation. These are too numerous to list. Your local bookseller will stock a wide range. Alternatively your local library will carry many titles and will be able to order others for you.

My Reference List
••••••••••••••••••••••••••••••

Use this space to keep notes of useful titles you come across during your job search. Photocopy this page and insert additional sheets if you need them.

Title:

Author:

Publisher:

Details – on order/collection date etc . . .

••••••••••••••

Title:

Author:

Publisher:

Details:

Title:

Author:

Publisher:

Details:

My Contacts List
·······························

Use this section to keep a note of your own contacts. You can photocopy the pages and insert them if you need more. Remember to enter the date of your contact so that you can write or phone them again between 8 and 10 weeks later.

Contact Name:

Position:

Organisation:

Address:

Telephone Number:

Date contact made: Date of next contact:

Additional Notes:

········

Contact Name:

Position:

Organisation:

Address:

Telephone Number:

Date contact made: Date of next contact:

Additional Notes:

Contact Name:

Position:

Organisation:

Address:

Telephone Number:

Date contact made: Date of next contact:

Additional Notes:

Contact Name:

Position:

Organisation:

Address:

Telephone Number:

Date contact made: Date of next contact:

Additional Notes:

Notes

Use the following pages for any additional notes you need to make during your job search.